Theology Today
32 Theology of the Priesthood

Theology Today

GENERAL EDITOR:
EDWARD YARNOLD, S.J.

No. 32

The Theology
of the Priesthood

BY

PAUL EDWARDS, S.J.

distributed by
CLERGY BOOK SERVICE
HALES CORNERS, WISCONSIN

ISBN 0-85342-420-9

Nihil Obstat:
Mgr. F. G. Thomas, S.T.L.
24 October 1974

Imprimatur
Mgr. D. Leonard, V.G.
Birmingham, 24 October 1974

Cum licentia superiorum ordinis

ACKNOWLEDGEMENTS

Thanks are due to the Division of Christian Education of the National Council of the Churches of Christ in the U.S.A. for the Scripture quotations from the *Revised Standard Version of the Bible*, copyrighted 1946 and 1952; also to the America Press and Geoffrey Chapman, Ltd., London, for quotations from *The Documents of Vatican II* (ed. W.M. Abbott, S.J.).

ABBREVIATION

Dz   H. Denzinger & A. Schönmetzer, *Enchiridion Symbolorum, Definitionum et Declarationum* (33rd edit., Barcelona etc., 1965)

CONTENTS

PREFACE

Catholic theology has been slow to attempt a clarification of the theology of priesthood. Vatican II, with its decree *Presbyterorum Ordinis*, has gone some of the way towards filling the need, though some will feel that there is still much to be said, especially on the relationship between the celebration of the Mass and the priest's other pastoral duties.

But the unresolved problems are not only theological. There are others—not unconnected with the theological ones—which might be described as sociological. How, for example, should priests spend their time? Should they, or may they, also undertake secular jobs? If so, do they do this as part of their priestly work, or is it a separate occupation? In other words, are they part-time or hyphenated priests? Should a priest be a man set apart from his fellows? If so, should he announce this fact by a distinctive dress and life-style?

The theological and sociological questions cannot be answered without a knowledge of the history of the Christian priesthood. One of Fr. Edwards' qualifications for his task is his training as a historian. His friends and readers will recognise with pleasure his distinctive blend of humour and good-natured combativeness; but those who are meeting him for the first time should not let his lightness of touch hide the fact that this is a serious and well-informed treatment of a very important subject.

E. J. Yarnold, S.J.

PRELIMINARY

'When were you ordained, Paul?', asked a young fellow priest. Preferring, as always, the resonant phrase to the simple factual statement, I replied, 'I was ordained in the year of Her Majesty's coronation.' 'I wish I could say that,' commented the curate, a patriotic Englishman in a diocese manned predominantly by Irishmen.

As I strive to bring this little work to birth the twentieth anniversary of that ordination is a few weeks away, and I see my efforts as a gesture of thanksgiving for those twenty years.

The other works in this series are written with an admirably austere objectivity. On the grounds of the twentieth anniversary of my ordination I ask the reader's, not to say the editor's, indulgence for a more personal presentation of my material. Assuming that indulgence, I proceed. . . .

Chapter 1

INTRODUCTION

A well known clerical outfitter used to send me his annual catalogue, the illustrations in which intrigued me greatly. The most striking were the coloured ones at the back. They showed gently smirking prelates garbed rather like Santa Claus, but with the unbecoming additions of an antimacassar round their hips and a purple silk biretta on their heads. Sufficiently entertained, and sometimes irritated, by this picturesque and preposterous parade, I would turn to the contrasting figures of the lower clergy. These were birds of a very different plumage, dimly and uniformly subfusc.

The prelates plainly, or rather very ornately, represent, albeit in pantomine fashion, an aristocracy, while the priests, plainly — in both senses of the word — belong to the Third Estate. Not, of course, to the labouring classes, but to the bourgeoisie. Their clothing, the collars and stocks apart, would suit the conservative bank manager, the modestly prosperous lawyer, the middle ranking civil servant. Their expressions are very interesting. They look educated, but not especially intelligent, nor deeply wise. They are smoothly bland. They look competent, but not vigorous. These men have not mastered their passions; they have been bred without them. They are as inoffensive as dehorned cows.

I am being a little fanciful. When did the lineaments of a tailor's model proclaim wisdom, vigour or the harrowing knowledge of good and evil? All the same, advertisements are normally revealing. They will commonly present an idealised customer as the real customer would very much like to see himself. An astute advertiser holds up an obsequious mirror to our wishful thinking, and the clerical outfitter's catalogue undoubtedly catches certain facets of the clerical world. In the first place it definitely establishes that world as a world in some degree apart. This is the reason for the clerical outfit; they are different, and so dress differently. But they are not apart as a convent of Trappists or a commune of hippies might be. They want to be accepted by society and so aim at a socially acceptable exterior. They have a function in that society and their clothes proclaim that distinct function, while placing them in a stratum with other functionaries, the medical man, the lawyer, the accountant — this, of course, before a degree of trendiness became allowable. These are respectable professions claiming respect because they require a good general education, reinforced by a specific training, and because they involve a fair degree of responsibility. They are respectable too in the less pleasant sense of that word, rather more prosperous than the working class, somewhat more dignified, or should I say solemn, as befits the 'responsible', the worthy, the influential citizen.

There is nothing of the visionary, the prophetic, the other-worldly in my clerical outfitter's models. But they do have an air of benevolence, a bland civility, a proper modesty of bearing, all entirely becoming. Evangelical zeal, ardent charity, profound humility have been tamed, and their domestic, suburban transmutations become entirely comfortable to live with.

But the outfitter's catalogue is meant to be the starting point of an enquiry into who and what these distinctively, conservatively garbed men may be, and not the basis of a sermon at a priests' retreat. For the moment I want to start another hare, which, I hope, will lead us eventually in the same direction.

Once when I was a small boy coming home to dinner from school I met a local priest, looking much like one of the models in the catalogue, but after the clothes had had twelve months wear. A well trained child, I politely pulled the peak of my cap down (paradoxically this process of pulling one's cap down was known as 'raising one's cap'), and said 'Good morning, Father.' The priest, pleased with my respectful greeting, stopped, asked me a few questions about myself and, in his pleasure, gave me a penny. This was the strict, literal equivalent of my week's pocket money. Over my dinner I told my mother about meeting the priest. At teatime, when my father came home from work, he was told how Paul had talked to a priest and been given a penny by him. 'Of course,' said my father, 'you mustn't spend it.' My money box was opened, the penny identified (which shows you how few coins were there), and my father took out his penknife and put scratches across the coin so as to distinguish it from its commonplace companions, and preserve it from the ignominious fate of being spent. That penny, which the priest gave me, remained in my money box for years, until my mother, hastily raiding my money box for change to pay the coalman, failed to remember the penny's sacred character, and so passed it into the coalman's blackened palm. But the memory of the whole event has never passed, and the recollection of my father scratching marks in that penny because the priest had given it to me, is as fresh as the scratches were on the day he did them. That incident sums up neatly the old-fashioned reverence of the simple Catholic for the priest.

In the next scene I am forty years older. It is late on a Saturday night in the Chaplain's office. I had come in to discuss the next day's Masses with the Chaplain. In the room was an intelligent postgraduate student, a woman in her twenties reading theology. At the moment she was not studying theology, but thoughtfully drinking the Chaplain's whisky. She had some sort of right to be drinking the Chaplain's whisky because she was a very generous supporter of the Chaplaincy and a good friend to both of us. We were pursuing our clerical discussion when she interrupted us. 'I hate priests', she said.

I believe that my father's reverence for priests and Miss Theology Student's dislike shared a common basis. For my father, priests were special people who represented God, who represented the Church—in fact were the Church—who taught in the name of God and distributed his sacraments. For Miss T.S. also, priests were a special brand of men, who told her what she should believe, what she should do, while their control of the Church put her, not only in a position of inferiority, but of impotence. She keenly resented what my father deeply respected.

My father's veneration, Miss T.S.'s alienation and the clerical outfitter's catalogue come together quite neatly. All three envisage the cleric as a member of a distinct caste deserving special respect or special dislike, and requiring special clothes. But those clothes, while distinctive, are not completely *sui generis;* as I have already said, they resemble the rig of an old fashioned G.P. or family lawyer. The clothes are alike because the status of the wearers is roughly the same. Medicine is the business of the physician, the law that of the lawyer, while the cleric deals with religion. Each is the custodian of his own 'mysteries'; for each of them the outsider is a mere 'layman'.

Miss T.S. having had a Catholic upbringing spoke of 'priests'. The Englishman 'in the street' would be more likely to use the word 'clergyman', but would speak of a clergyman whom he knew to be a Catholic as a 'priest'. Outside the Roman Catholic body, the use of the word is a reasonably safe index of the theological distance from Rome. Anglo-Catholics use the word habitually; the middle-of-the-road Anglican much less, while one is surprised to hear a Non-conformist apply it to his minister. Since the Reformation the word 'priesthood' is associated with Popery, with the Mass, with an elaborate sacramental system, with intricate ritual. The word almost carries with it a whiff of incense.

The word is used in the context of other religions on much the same basis. It is uncommon to speak of a Moslem 'priest' because we associate the mosque with oral prayer rather than ceremonial. But the word commonly occurs when we are speaking of Hinduism, because their worship is ritualistic and complex. We always speak of Egyptian, Jewish, Greek and Roman priests, because they had temples and sacrifices. The word 'priest' suggests ritual worship with a whole background of ceremonial props; it implies a distinct caste, who alone may carry out the rituals; it implies the power and status conferred by this monopoly of the sacred. The word 'priest' used of the reverend gentlemen in their Roman collars and clerical gabardines, makes them the colleagues of the priests of Apollo and Baal, of Kali and Kybele, of Odin and Osiris. They would

12

look out of place greeting the winter solstice (although on second thoughts, Midnight Mass comes close to it). One cannot imagine them manipulating the sacrificial knife with any aplomb, yet they are thought of as a Western European equivalent of those pagan mystagogues. They may take Benediction and not the auspices; their incense may come in tins, but they are considered to have the same monopoly of the sacred (awesome to my father; hateful to Miss T.S.), and that makes them people apart, that apartness being proclaimed in their dress. And hence my clerical outfitter's catalogue.

The gentlemen in the illustrations, even the youngest of them, would answer to the title 'Father'. This does much to explain their manner and expression. They are Victorian fathers (it was during the reign of the Great Queen that English speaking Catholics learned to address their priests as 'Father') of the milder sort, dignified, reliable, solicitous, acting only from the best motives in the interests of those for whom they are responsible.

The man chiefly responsible for the adoption of the style 'Father' by the English diocesan clergy was Cardinal Manning. In 1883 Cardinal Manning published a book, *The Eternal Priesthood*. In 1951 Monsignor H.F. Davis said, 'It would be hard to find another work on the priesthood regarded with equal reverence, unless it be one of the classics of antiquity ... whatever may be the fate of his other works, one at least, his *Eternal Priesthood* will continue to inspire many generations of future priests'. In 1964, the Second Vatican Council rendered the Cardinal's approach to the subject obsolete. Manning wrote, 'There can be conceived no office higher, and no power greater than the office of a priest'. For him 'the priesthood was complete ... (when) the pastoral authority and world-wide commission of the Apostles were not yet given.' Vatican II explicitly reverses this. In the Dogmatic Constitution of the Church the Council begins with the people of God; then it sets forth the hierarchical structure of the Church, which, of course, is mainly concerned with the episcopacy. The priest has his incidental mention in such phrases as 'with their helpers, the priests and deacons' and 'the bishops for whom the priests are assistants'. The decree which deals explicitly with the priesthood, 'Presbyterorum Ordinis', does the same thing at greater length and even more pointedly. Parts of it could be read as an intentional refutation of Cardinal Manning.

The shift in perspective between Cardinal Manning's view of the priesthood and that of Vatican II is so extreme as to amount almost to a Copernican Revolution. The momentum of this transition has carried thinkers far beyond the position of the Council, while leaving others almost at the starting point. So I have in recent years read articles calling upon the clergy to bear 'the stamp of today and tomorrow', and even to 'build socialism', while the ordination address I sat through this summer completely ignored the declarations of Vatican II.

If, then, I ask who are those gentlemen in clerical clothes, still more if I ask who they are meant to be, and what they ought to become, I shall get answers ranging from the neo-mediaeval to the futurological.

Chapter 2

BACK TO MELCHIZEDEK

Cardinal Manning relished a fullbodied phrase. The quotation he most liked to deploy for the benefit of his clergy was, 'Thou art a priest for ever according to the order of Melchizedek'. Melchizedek can be rolled round the tongue almost like a necromancer's word of power. The Church is fond of quoting the Old Testament. A Catholic bride used to have a whole litany of Old Testament heroines intoned over her head, and the priest being ordained heard not only of Moses and Aaron but also of Eleazar and Ithamar. (Ithamar? yes, Ithamar!)

This use of the Old Testament can be sheer embellishment. The Old Testament writers were good storytellers, and their heroic figures are really memorable (but not Ithamar!). The recitation of Old Testament names can give to prayer a fine religious sonority. If more than that is intended, then the Old Testament needs to be used very carefully. It is important. It is the word of God. It provided the notions, the archetypal figures, the principal frame of reference in which the minds of Jesus and his Jewish contemporaries functioned. For this last reason alone, its bearing on the New Testament can seldom, if ever, be ignored. At the same time we have in any particular scriptural context to try and reckon with the degree of development between the two Testaments, a degree of development which might sometimes be an abrupt transformation.

On the subject of the New Testament ministry, there are writers who seem to find the Old Testament precedents to be much more obscuring than illuminating and therefore omit them. But Old Testament parallels have been quoted concerning the Christian minister, as far back as Clement in the first century. That such quotations have often confused rather than clarified seems to me a good reason for facing the issue. Everyone knows that priesthood, as conceived in terms of sacrifice, of altars, of incense and ritual, bulks large in the Old Testament. It is often referred to as the Aaronic priesthood. 'Then bring near to you Aaron your brother, and his sons with him, from among the people of Israel to serve me as priests' (Exod 28.1). It may need pointing out that the responsibilities of the priesthood were not entirely ceremonial. In Deuteronomy Levi is charged with the care of the oracle, the teaching of the law and lastly the offering of incense and holocausts (Deut 33. 8-10). As the oracle was meant to reveal the will of Yahweh, and the instruction in the law was a more elaborate form of communicating that will, the priest's responsibility is quite as much to guide the people as to perform the rituals for them. In the later composition, Malachi, the priests are severely taken to task for their failures in this respect. 'For the lips of the priest should guard knowledge, and men should seek instruction from his mouth, for he is the messenger of the Lord of Hosts. But you have turned aside from the way; you have caused many to stumble' (Mal 2. 7,8).

So the priests are more than cultic officials. But there are further complications. Aaron, as we saw above, was to be the priest and the source of priests. But when Yahweh makes the covenant with Israel, it is Moses who builds the altar, who spills the blood of the sacrifices half upon the altar and half upon the people (Exod 24. 4-8). Moses here plays the role of high-priest at a ceremony of much greater significance than any which Aaron or his progeny would perform.

Then there were the kings of Israel. With our late Western European background, we tend to think of the king wielding political secular authority, while the priests exercise religious authority. We forget the elaborate religious rite with which the Queen was crowned twenty years ago. We also forget that Israel was a religious community, to be defined largely in terms of religious belief and practice. The leader of such a people was necessarily a religious figure. For this reason he was solemnly anointed — as was Her Majesty twenty years ago.

The king is also a cultic figure. This is quite confusing. When Saul dares to offer sacrifice, although with every extenuating circumstance, he is severely censured (1 Sam 13).

16

Yet when the ark of the covenent was brought to Jerusalem, David presided over the whole affair. 'And when David had finished offering the burnt offerings and the peace offerings, he blessed the people in the name of the Lord of hosts' (2 Sam 6, 18). But that event was completely outclassed by the later transference of the same ark to Solomon's new temple. And on this occasion Solomon presides. 'Now as Solomon finished offering all this prayer and supplication to the Lord, he arose from before the altar of the Lord, where he had knelt with hands outstretched towards heaven, and he stood and blessed all the assembly of Israel' (1 Kings 8. 54). So not only are the kings credited with initiating, planning and providing for these historic religious occasions, they are described as playing the star roles. If the kings were not high-priests in name and theory, they look like super-priests in practice.

We have seen that the priests had a charge other than the purely ceremonial, that they were responsible for making known the wishes of Yahweh. There is, of course, another group in Israel who communicate God's wishes, the prophets, the men to whom the 'word of the Lord' came. As dramatic personalities the prophets, such as Samuel (who, it must be admitted, acts as a priest as well), Nathan, Elijah and Elisha, utterly outclass the priests we meet in the Old Testament, and the prophetic literature is much more stirring than the legal codes associated with the priesthood. Yet dramatic quality is not the most reliable index of religious importance. Perhaps the priestly instruction dealt with everyday or at least commonly recurring situations, while the charismatic (that word cannot be wholly suppressed) intervention of the prophets was more appropriate to the individual and critical situation.

After the Jews, or some of them, returned from exile in Babylon and laboriously re-established themselves in Judea, prophecy seems to have atrophied. A new class of men became prominent, the scribes. These men were the scholars of Judaism, learned in 'the law' and zealous in teaching it. The Christian will normally underrate these men because the gospels depict their many clashes with Jesus. The gospel presentation is polemical, and does not do justice to their positive achievement, nor to the concern for righteousness by which they were possessed. Although they come into prominence as the prophets fade from the scene, the industry of the scribe was no substitute for the divine élan of the prophet. It is not the role of the prophet which the scribe takes over, rather the teaching role of the priest, confining the latter to his ceremonial activities.

What emerges from this brief survey? If we understand 'priesthood' in the general sense of a caste which performs the cult, which is associated with altar, incense and hieratic insignia, then there was such a priesthood among the Jews. But the picture is fuzzy. We think of Moses as the leader and Aaron as the priest, but, as we have seen, Moses plays the sacerdotal role at the ratification of the Covenant. Similarly, on the historic occasions concerning the Ark and Jerusalem, the Ark and the Temple, David and Solomon take over (do I make an illicit assumption when I say 'take over'?) the principal ceremonial role. If we look in the Old Testament not only for ministers of the cult but for all who held positions of religious leadership and responsibility, then we have to reckon with kings, prophets and later, scribes. There are no neat pigeon holes. Into which category does Moses fit? He leads like a king; as the medium of the 'word of the Lord' he is surely the greatest of the prophets, and at the most significant ceremony of all, he is the high-priest of Israel. Samuel seems predominantly a seer, but offers sacrifice and anoints kings. The major prophet Ezekiel was a priest. There seems to be an overlap between the duties of the priest to preserve and expound the law, and the labours of the scribes. It is all very unsatisfactory for somebody who likes to disentangle the past as neatly as he might dismantle a piece of meccano.

There is some interest, though perhaps no great theological profit, in measuring the life of Jesus against these. He was certainly not a priest. The priests were of the tribe of Levi, and he belonged to Juda. In the Temple he was a layman. Kingship, which included political authority and military leadership, he refused; he had not come to be another David fighting

Romans instead of Philistines. In as much as he taught and had disciples, he looks something like a scribe, but he was without their training and taught in a markedly different way. Perhaps he comes nearest to the prophets, and nearest of all to the great figure of Moses, who cannot be fitted into, or wholly excluded from, any of the categories. On second thoughts you can exclude Moses from the category of 'scribe'.

Out of deference to Cardinal Manning, I should like to glance at Melchizedek. He has two verses of the Abram story. He is described there as King of Salem and priest of God Most High. Then there is the intriguing verse which Manning so loved to quote from Ps 110. This is very obscure. Most of the psalm is addressed to a king. If verse 4, 'You are a priest for ever after the order of Melchizedek', is so addressed, then we see once again the priestly character of the King. But it is also suggested that the psalm is an imaginary dialogue between David and Zadok, and that in this verse David is confirming Zadok in his priesthood, not, strangely enough, the Aaronic priesthood, but in succession from Melchizedek, the ancient Canaanite King of Jerusalem.

In sum, in the Old Testament, there are priests of the knife and incense variety. But religious responsibility, religious leadership, takes a variety of forms, which are not entirely distinct from one another, and which do not remain unchanged throughout Israel's history. Add the undeniable fact that the institutions of Israel do not necessarily survive into the Christian Church, that if they do survive, there is good reason to expect them to be radically transformed, and we seem to be left with the Old Testament throwing no light whatever on the Christian ministry.

I do not know whether one could call it 'light', but the above facts do raise a question in my mind. The eminent philosopher Descartes aimed at 'clear and distinct ideas'. Quite rightly so. But the quest for clarity and precision may lead us to impose on reality a neatness and simplicity which are not there. Human relationships are often vague and shifting. Therefore to put them into lucidly clear and sharply distinct categories is to misrepresent them. So I ask myself: if under the Old Law the forms of religious authority and religious responsibility were somewhat indeterminate, varying with the course of Israel's history, is there any compelling *a priori* reason why under the New Dispensation the forms of religious authority and responsibility should be neatly and plainly distinguishable from one another, or any reason why those forms should be utterly immutable throughout the Church's history and future development?

Chapter 3

A PROFUSION OF PRESBYTERS

In the Old Testament, the pattern of distribution of religious leadership and responsibility is far from clear; but the New Testament picture of the organisation, if that word applies, of the early Church, is twice as baffling. But in the confusion, one fact is quite clear. You cannot find any priests, if by priests you mean a distinct caste, easily identifiable, adepts of incense and altar, the denizens of the sanctuary. The Greek word for the cultic priest is '*hiereus*'. In the New Testament the word is used for the Jewish priest. But it is applied to no individual in the Christian congregations, nor to any group within the Church. We read of the 'twelve', of 'apostles' (not quite the same thing as the former), of the 'seven', of 'bishops' (in what sense remains to be discussed), of 'elders' (who will have to be discussed beyond the point of tedium), of deacons, of prophets, evangelists, pastors, teachers, miracle-workers, healers and helpers, of administrators and of speakers in tongues (1 Cor 12. 28 and 1 Thess 5. 12). But nowhere priests! Perhaps one could re-edit the New Testament and call it 'His Reverence Vanishes' or 'The Disappearing Priest' or — my own favourite — 'The Mystery of the Missing Mystagogue'.

It has been said that this absence of the word 'priest' indicates a deliberate rejection by the Christians of the whole institution of priesthood; e.g. 'Only 2,000 years ago, there was a small community who on the ground of a new insight, realised that the priesthood for man is an incredible failure and nonsense' (Tibor Horvath in *Theology of a New Diaconate*). Trenchantly rhetorical and appealingly radical but, not, I think, soundly based. One should not draw conclusions about what the early Christians 'realised' merely because a certain term was not employed by them. Nor should one forget how slow the New Israel of the Christian Church was in breaking with the institutions of the Old. The first Christians went to the Temple daily. There was deep heartsearching be-

21

fore they abandoned circumcision and decided not to require full observance of the 'Mosaic' code from the gentile converts. As late as 58 A.D., Paul regarded it as a serious accusation that he had taught 'all the Jews who are among the Gentiles to forsake Moses, telling them not to circumcise their children or observe the customs' (Acts 21.21). To rebut the charge Paul, having been introduced to four Christians who were 'under a vow', 'took the men, and the next day he purified himself with them, and went into the Temple to give notice when the days of purification would be fulfilled and the offering presented for every one of them' (Acts 21.26). Are we to think that the early Christians revered and frequented the temple while despising its priesthood? Is it not a great deal more likely that they continued for a long time to accept the sanctity and validity of the temple and its priesthood, as the Lord Jesus, in his lifetime, an observant Jew, had accepted them?

The umbilical cord between Israel and the Church was not abruptly severed on the day of Pentecost. The Church took time to realise that it had its own set of organs, entirely capable of sustaining its own independent spiritual life. But did the new organism include the priesthood?

In the Church as we see it in the New Testament, living, moving developing — and we must remember that our picture is fragmentary — there is a profusion of terms and titles. There are 'the Twelve', an important body, a very important body, but one essentially evanescent, by reason of its requirement that its members should 'have accompanied us during all the time that the Lord Jesus went in and out among us' (Acts 1.21). There are 'apostles'. One grew up hearing of the twelve Apostles, but soon learned that Paul, not one of the Twelve, ranked as an apostle. But it required a more sophisticated acquaintance with the New Testament to know that the term is also used of Barnabas (Acts 14.14), of the otherwise unknown Andronicus and Junias (Rom 16.7), and to be aware that James 'the Lord's brother', spoken of as an Apostle (Gal. 1.19), is not reckoned by exegetes to have been one of the Twelve. Does the word have the same sense in all contexts? A moderately clear concept of Apostleship, which would overlap with the mission and responsibility of the Twelve, but which would stretch to cover James and Paul, can be constructed. As this concept would include the assertion that the office is the 'basic constitutive element of the Church', it is of primary importance in an ecclesiology, yet must not at present delay us as we scan each avenue for our evaporated priest. The search might be easier if each avenue did not turn into quite a different one in the course of the investigation. Thus in Acts 6, seven men are specially appointed 'to serve tables', to spare the Twelve for 'prayer and the ministry of the word'. But the story of their appointment is followed by the account of Stephen, one of the seven, preaching with such effect as to bring about his arrest, trial and martyrdom, and Philip, another of the seven, is soon evangelising Samaria. In Acts 21.3 he is described as Philip, 'the evangelist, who was one of the seven'. The serving of tables has been transmuted into the ministry of the word!

The choosing of the seven is interesting because of the communal participation in the process. 'And the twelve summoned the body of the disciples and said, ". . . Therefore, brethren, pick out from among you some men of good repute. . . ." And what they said pleased the whole multitude and they chose. . . . These they set before the Apostles and they prayed and laid their hands on them' (Acts 6. 2-6). As numbers grew, such communal conduct of affairs could not have lasted. So when the church at Antioch had been established and developed to the point where it was able to send financial help to the Jerusalem Church, 'they did so sending it to the elders by the hands of Barnabas and Saul' (Acts 11. 30). A new organ of responsibility has emerged, and the word 'elders' becomes a familiar one. When the crucial debate about circumcision erupted, Paul and Barnabas 'were appointed to go up to Jerusalem to the apostles and elders about this question' (15. 2). The elders are involved at every stage of the subsequent discussion. 'The apostles and elders were gathered together to consider the matter' (v.6). The final decree goes out from 'The brethren, both apostles and elders, to the brethren who are of the gentiles . . .' (v. 24).

At that Council of Jerusalem, as it is often called, James, whose prestige we have already commented on, seems to act as chairman. He does so more clearly when Paul makes his final visit to Jerusalem. 'Paul went in with us to James; and all the elders were present' (Acts 21.18). Apparently the church at Jerusalem had evolved a management committee, a body of 'elders' under the presidency of James. It is down this particular avenue that we may find our vanished priest, or his nearest equivalent. The avenue is neither straight nor narrow; it may even be a group of interconnected avenues. It has often seemed to me more of a maze than anything else. So into the maze with courage and compass, not to say 'forks and hope'.

Biblical commentators learnedly tell us that councils of elders governed Hittite towns, and enjoyed judicial power in Babylon. One takes off one's hat to such erudition, and yet finds it a little narrow in its Near Eastern concern. The matter, I think, deserves a broader context. A human community may manage its affairs in a mass assembly as the first Christians seem to have done in choosing the seven, as a kibbutz does today. This required manageable numbers and very strong convictions about equality. A community may hand over a good deal of authority to a single individual. This is more likely to occur when the community is large, and when cohesion and control are urgently necessary. In such circumstances the Hebrew tribes, preyed upon by Amalekites, Ammonites and Arameans and especially the Philistines, accepted the monarchy of Saul. But there is a third possibility in which authority is exercised by a group. Sometimes a whole nation has managed its affairs in this way, as did the United Provinces of the Netherlands in the seventeenth century. But the system is best suited to a smaller entity, such as a district or town. Have not town councils been the commonest form of urban government? Sometimes monarchy is diluted by the co-presence of a responsible group, e.g. King and Parliament.

But let us think rather of a more elementary stage of political development. When a select group exercises leadership and authority over a larger community, the members of the select group will belong to it because of some special source of prestige, perhaps sheer seniority, perhaps experience, personal prowess or property. At a very elementary stage, the natural leaders of the community are the patriarchal heads of families, quite literally the 'elders'. The term survives into a very different age and acquires a very different sense, cf. the English word 'alderman'. In the history of Israel the term 'elders' has a rich variety of applications. Moses complained 'I am not able to carry all this people alone' (Num 11.14). He was told, 'Gather for me seventy men of the elders of Israel, who you know to be the elders of the people and officers over them. .... And I will take some of the spirit which is upon you and put it upon them' (*ibid.* 16, 17). When David was working his protection racket and had a particularly large windfall, 'he sent part of the spoil to his friends, the elders of Judah' (1 Sam 30. 26). These would seem to be the heads of clans and families within the tribe. When the monarchy is an established institution, we hear of 'the elders of the land'. Here the phrase would seem to cover those men of local importance and influence, whom no king could afford to alienate.

To come to the time of the Roman occupation and a little nearer to the days of the nascent Church. It is said that at this period all Jewish communities, whether in Palestine or in cities outside Palestine, had their own ruling councils of 'elders', one of their principal functions being to deal for their people with the gentile authorities. Synagogues were managed by such councils of 'elders'. In Jerusalem the great 'Council' or Sanhedrin was composed of priests, elders and scribes, the scribes being comparatively late-comers to the institution. Jesus was arrested by Judas with a posse 'from the chief priests and elders of the people' (Mt. 26. 47). Then he was taken 'to Caiaphas, the high priest, where the scribes and elders had gathered' (26. 57).

The term 'elders' did a great deal of work in the course of time. It would come very high on Humpty-Dumpty's Saturday night wage-scale. But its labours did not end with the Sanhedrin and synagogue. When Christian missionaries had made sufficient converts to establish a congregation, they could hardly, when the time came for them to move off, leave their body of converts 'unstructured'. So Paul and Barnabas returned from their first missionary journey, leaving their new-founded churches only 'when they had appointed elders for them in every church with prayers and fasting' (Acts 14.13). Of course, we have already met the word 'elders' in a Christian context as used of the officials of the Jerusalem church.

But simple consistency of terminology is, as always, too much to hope for. When Paul was on his way back to Jerusalem after his third missionary safari, 'he sent to Ephesus and called to him the elders of the church' (Acts 20.17). The Greek word for elders is *presbyteroi*. But in his address to the dutifully assembled elders, St Paul says (v.28) that the Holy Spirit has made them *episcopoi*, 'guardians' or 'overseers', the ancestor of our word 'bishop'. Whatever the later relationship of priest and bishop, *de facto* or *de jure*, in this chapter of the Acts, *presbyteroi* and *episcopoi* are plainly equivalents.

So they are in many other places in the New Testament. The letter to the Philippians greets the 'saints in Christ Jesus who are at Philippi with the *episcopoi* and deacons'. In some manuscripts of 1 Pet 5.2 the presbyters are described as *'episcopountes'*, 'bishoping' (!). The first Letter to Timothy (1 Tim 3.1) lists the qualities needed in an *episcopos* and in the deacons, without mention of *presbyteroi*. The Letter to Titus (Tit 1.5) tells him to appoint 'elders in every town' and gives a long list of requisite characteristics, and says in the course of the list 'for an *episcopos*, as God's steward, must be. ...' Hence the terms *presbyteros* and *episcopos* seem interchangeable labels for the same office.

The case is not so crushingly cogent that all accept it. It is pointed out that the word *episcopos* usually occurs in the singular, as though there were only one per church, which is to assume that the singular is not merely generic. It is considered relevant that some of the Qumran camps (it is *de rigueur* to make some mention of Qumran when describing a New Testament subject) had an official, a single official, called an 'overseer', whose title and responsibilities seem to correspond to those of the *episcopos*. It is also suggested that some of the

26

qualities demanded in the *episcopos* in 1 Tim 3.1-7 would fit a single individual better than one of a group; e.g. 'he must be well thought of by outsiders' (v.7) would apply strongly to one man representing the Christian community.

All this is a little thin, but we are on solid ground when we remember that the Jerusalem elders had a clearly pre-eminent president in James. Besides, one can hardly imagine any committee functioning without some sort of chairman. The situation probably varied from community to community. Some congregations were largely Jewish in origin; others largely Gentile. There would be different degrees of contact with an Apostle, with itinerant organisers such as Timothy and Titus, with some mother church. The less a community was directed from outside, the greater the responsibility thrust upon the presiding presbyter. It is certainly a very feasible hypothesis that as a local church became more self-reliant, the presidency of that church evolved into an office distinct from the presbyterate as a whole, and that the term *episcopos* came to be used of the chairman. But the surest fact in the whole matter is that homogeneity of structure and terminology is neither to be found nor looked for.

Because the messages in the second and third chapters of Revelation are sent 'to the angel of the church' in Ephesus, in Smyrna and so on, it has been alleged that these communities had a presiding presbyter-bishop and that he is the 'angel'. This is sheer conjecture. Revelation has some splendid elders. 'Round the throne were twenty-four thrones, and seated on the thrones were twenty-four elders, clad in white garments, with golden crowns upon their heads' (Apoc 4. 4); 'the twenty-four elders fell down before the Lamb, each holding a harp, and with golden bowls full of incense, which are the prayers of the saints' (Apoc 5. 8).

Because these elders are grouped round the throne, and the liturgy of a later generation grouped the presbyters round the bishop, it is suggested that at the time of the book's composition the liturgy was already so celebrated in the churches of that area. But the work is so highly imaginative, so densely metaphorical that such factual conclusions seem out of place.

One piece of information can be distilled from these passages. The gorgeous elders, throned, crowned, arrayed in white, equipped with harps, are at least in part sacerdotal figures, in that they offer incense and present the prayers of the saints, and therefore the word 'elders' can admit of sacerdotal associations; it is not so intransigently secular as to reject any touch of the priestly. And that, as we are looking for priests, is just as well!

Chapter 4

ECCE SACERDOS MAGNUS

I see that at this point I am in real danger of attempting to write a century by century history of the Church. Resisting the temptation I am going to attempt something which may well prove harder, to sum up in one magisterial paragraph the history of the episcopacy and the priesthood, from the end of the New Testament period down to the time of my own ordination. ('May the Lord help you!' says a passing colleague, to whom I have just confided this bold, not to say hubristic, decision.)

In the second and third centuries, predominantly in the second, the local Christian churches came to be presided over by a single individual called the bishop, assisted by presbyter and deacons. To the bishop, or rather to the episcopal order as a whole, the patristic age attributed immense significance. The bishops are the successors of the Apostles; the presbyters but auxiliaries of the bishop. Of both bishop and presbyter the old cultic, sacerdotal terminology, drawn from the Old Testament or the Graeco-Roman religions, comes to be used quite as a matter of course. This is part of a growing 'clericalisation'. The Christian minister becomes differentiated from the laity in dress, title and social obligations, while the laity are reduced to the role of taught, 'ministered to' and governed.

Then (I have decided to cut my masterly paragraph in two) a most intriguing development took place, spreading over many centuries. The Fathers had established the bishop in a key role, which the theological speculation of centuries then eroded to something like vanishing point. The sacramental powers of the bishop, so theologians decided, fall within the essential, radical competence of the presbyter. The bishop's jurisdiction, so papalising theologians judged, derived from the Holy See. What then of substance was left to give the concept of 'bishop' any real body? Nothing, apparently! My own teacher on the subject of the sacrament of Orders held that a priest was a 'suppressed' bishop, his ordination conferring on him the same powers as a bishop has, but not giving him the permission to use them. Before I was ordained a priest (or, in the views of my lecturer in sacramental theology, a 'suppressed' bishop) I was briefly a deacon, because that office had withered to a mere ritual, prefatory to the priesthood. The real diaconate was a thousand years dead. With the genuine diaconate defunct, and the bishop theologised out of independent existence, the ministry into which I was ordained seemed to consist of the Pope and a multitude of priests, a minority of the latter being allowed to exercise their power to ordain and to confirm, and being required to supervise the work of other priests, in patches of territory called dioceses.

Without writing an entire church history, I must try to show some of the steps by which this situation was reached. When Clement of Rome was writing to the Christians at Corinth towards the end of the first century A.D., the words *episcopos* and *presbyteros* were still interchangeable. The government of the church in Corinth would appear to be collegial. But a very different structure is seen in the letters written by St. Ignatius of Antioch (died c.117) to a group of churches in Asia Minor. There is a single *episcopos*, a plainly dominant figure, the centre of unity, whose concurrence is necessary in all things, with the presbyters and deacons playing their valuable but subordinate, concordant roles. Here there is no mention of itinerant apostles, of prophets, or of 'teachers'. This is not to say this particular structure was already the universal pattern. But it was on the road to becoming so.

Less than a century after the martyrdom of Ignatius (perhaps in the amphitheatre at Rome) Irenaeus, bishop of Lyons, died, probably a martyr too, though in less picturesque circumstances. Irenaeus was brought up in Asia Minor, and in his youth knew men who had known the Apostle John. He spent much of his life in Gaul, and knew Rome. He is therefore a very valuable witness both to Christian tradition and to contemporary Christian practice over a wide area. Even at this time the vocabulary can be confusing with the terms *episcopus* and *presbyter* (in the Latin this time) apparently equivalent in some contexts (e.g. *Adv. Haereses*, 4: 26: 2). But Irenaeus is normally dealing with individual presidents of churches, and placing great weight on the fact that they derive their office from the Apostles, and with the office a '*charisma veritatis*' (charism of truth: *Adv. Haer.* 4: 26: 2). The witness of those bishops who trace their sees back to the Apostles is his principal polemical weapon.

A generation later there is no ambiguity about the terms *episcopus* and *presbyter* for Hippolytus of Rome (d. 235). He has left us the prayers used in the ceremonies with which the bishop and presbyter were ordained. The difference in status is quite plain. The bishop is compared with a high priest; the presbyter is assimilated to the elders who assisted Moses. The presbyter is subordinate and subsidiary. One more generation, and we meet the supreme protagonist of the episcopal order, Cyprian of Carthage (d. 258): 'inde per temporum et successionem vices, episcoporum ordinatio et ecclesiae ratio decurrit, ut ecclesia super episcopos constituatur et omnis actus ecclesiae per eosdem praepositos gubernetur' (Letter 33) ('... the Church is founded on the bishops, and they are the leaders who direct all the acts of the Church.') He is conspicuously eloquent in Letter 66. 'Unde scire debes episcopum in ecclesia esse et ecclesiam in episcopo ... quando ecclesia ... sit utique connexa et cohaerentium sibi invicem sacerdotum glutino copulata'. 'So you should know (my own translation) that the bishop is where the church is, and the church where the bishop is ... as the church is, as it were, held together and united by a glue of mutually adhesive bishops.' Should I have said 'bishops'? The word *sacerdos* is the one the Romans used for their priests, the equivalent of *hiereus*, the word which is not used within the Christian communities in the New Testament.

The most compelling testimony to the status of the bishop in the theology of the Patristic age is that of the consecration formularies of the period. Whether they be Roman, or Byzantine, Coptic or Chaldaic, they are at one in their high conception of the office being conferred. The bishop is said to succeed to the kings, prophets and priests of the Old Testa-

31

ment, and his consecration answers to their anointing. The bishop continues the work and mission of Christ; he succeeds to the powers given to the Apostles; he is a ruler, a shepherd, a teacher and a high priest. The liturgies show a clear awareness that the bishops form a college, the *ordo episcopalis* into which the new bishop is received. The collegial significance of the rite is underlined by the practice of having several bishops to perform the ceremony. The Synod of Arles (314) wanted the consecrating bishop to have seven co-consecrators. Nicaea (325) asserts that all the bishops of a province should partake, and that the irreducible minimum is three bishops.

As a boy, still in the primary school, I was told that three bishops were required to consecrate a new bishop. I was also told that the two extras were there to ensure validity. I do not remember the word 'validity' being used, but it may have been, for my primary school was something of a theological forcing-ground. With one bishop, we were told, there was an outside possibility of his making some mistake in the form, or of having an inadequate intention. To prevent such a disaster as an invalidly ordained bishop, and to make assurance doubly sure, the consecrator had to have two other bishops with him. I am not being autobiographical once again just to lighten a stodgy chapter. This particular straw proclaims clearly the direction of the theological wind, and how that direction has changed. The requirement of the three bishops sprang from a concern for collegiality. In the course of time that concern became quite crowded out by an obsession with the mechanics of valid transmission of the sacraments, with indispensable 'matter', with the essential 'form', with the 'right' intention.

To return to the patristic age. During it the old cultic terminology was commonly applied to the Christian ministers. We have 'priests' again. We met them above in Cyprian. The Greek work *hiereus* is used in the *Mystagogic Catechesis* (what an exquisite title!) of Cyril of Jerusalem, dated by some c.348 but by others as much later in the century. By the end of the fourth century it was commonplace to use the words *sacerdos* in the West, or *hiereus* in the East, of the Christian bishop. Gradually the terms came to be used of the presbyter. But the word *sacerdos* never completely replaced *presbyter*, which still remains a normal canonical Latin term. And the word 'priest' in its various European forms such as 'pretre' and 'priester' and so on, is, of course, derived not from *sacerdos*, but from *presbyter*. I find it intriguing that the Anglo-Saxons used the word 'preost', formed from *presbyter*, for the Christian priest, and the word 'sacerd', clearly from *sacerdos*, for a pagan or Jewish priest. And I find it charmingly ironical that the word 'priest', now so redolent of the hieratic and cultic, should testify etymologically to the non-hieratic language of the early Church.

The application of hieratic terms to the Christian ministry was no abrupt reversal, but a gradual process. The Letter to the Hebrews, which we shall see again, treats of Jesus in cultic language, 'we have such a high priest, one who is seated at the right hand of the throne of the Majesty in heaven, a minister in the sanctuary' (Heb. 8. 1,2). The phrase from Exodus (19.6) 'a kingdom of priests' is applied to the Christian community as a whole in 1 Pet 2.9, in Apoc 1.6, and in Apoc 5.10. Clement of Rome (died c. 97) draws analogies between the Christian minister and Aaron, and between the Christian assemblies and the Temple worship. Ignatius of Antioch (d. 117), writing to the Philadelphians, speaks of 'one eucharist . . . one altar, as there is one bishop. . .' Justin, the apologist, writing in the mid second century, in his *Dialogue with Trypho*, a Jew, speaks of the eucharist as a sacrifice, a sacrifice like that offered by the Jews, but far more acceptable to God (*Dial*, 41). Half a century later, or less, Irenaeus applies the words of Malachi (1. 10, 11) to the Christian eucharist. From speaking of the eucharist as a sacrifice, it is but a short step to calling the president thereof a priest. The deep interest of the Christian theologians in the Old Testament, which they saw as pre-figuring their own dispensation, inevitably affected their terminology. So the eventual application of *sacerdos* and *hiereus* to the Christian minister is no sudden counter-revolution, but a clearly traceable evolution.

The later stages of that evolution took place in a context enormously changed from that of the earlier Christians, and the change of context produced an immense external transformation. Christianity had become at first a recognised religion within the Roman Empire, and then the dominant cult. So its rites became public. They also became magnificent with lights, incense and fine vestments, the magnificence centering, of course, upon the officiating minister rather than on the worshipping laity. To this ceremonial splendour was added social rank with its outward manifestations. The Church became a highly important body, numerous and influential. Again, the importance, influence and external éclat accrued to its officials, rather than to the rank and file. Here the words 'officiating' and 'officials' have come naturally to my biro, as they did not in speaking of the earlier Christian communities. So it happened in the Church. Roman terms of political and social differentiation became part of the vocabulary of the Christian Church. Thus 'ordo' which was used of the senators and knights, became the label for the Christian sacrament of Holy Orders. (The receptionist at the Dental Hospital who wrote on my card 'clerk of the holy order' was not so far out.) Other Roman terms thus adopted were *gradus*, *dignitas* and *auctoritas*. These words carried with them too much of their secular political and social meaning. They were, if I may say so, baptized, but not converted.

More tangible privileges granted to the clergy in the later Empire were exemption from certain burdensome forms of public service, and from many taxes. While the state granted the clergy solid privileges, the Church was imposing on them a new obligation, at first that of abstinence within marriage, and eventually celibacy. As the Christian minister was being seen increasingly in terms of his Aaronic predecessor he became obliged to a levitical purity. All Israel had to abstain in preparation for the ratification of the Covenant with Yahweh (Exod 19. 15). According to Leviticus (15. 16-18) any seminal emission rendered a man ritually unclean. Now in the New Israel a more stringent discipline was enacted. The prestige of monasticism may have played its part. So may the obvious advantage of having the growing possessions of the Church in the hands of men without family. At first it seems abstinence in marriage that was demanded, as by the Council of Elvira (A.D. 305) and the Synod of Rome (386). Eventually the Eastern Church required celibacy of its bishops, normally drawing its episcopacy from the monasteries, while the Western Church came to impose celibacy on both bishop and presbyter.

When the Roman Empire collapsed in the West, the Christian Church survived. Whereas the Christian clergy had shared in the civilisation of Rome, after the 'barbarian' immigrations, what was left of that civilisation was largely monopolised by the clergy. Learning, such as it was, the knowledge of administration, or what there was of it, belonged to them. Some of the clergy became temporal rulers. Ecclesiastical princedoms survived in Germany until after 1800. The long line of ecclesiastics who were Chancellors of England is more typical of the part played by ecclesiastics in the political history of Western Europe. Eminence of that sort was achieved only by a tiny minority. No doubt the bulk of the clergy were poor, scantily educated, and with influence only in the neighbourhood of the parish pump. (I wonder if that is an anachronism?) But the double sense of the English word 'clerical' reminds us that the clergy were the literate element in western society. When medical men and lawyers refer to those outside their own body as 'laymen', the same point is made. The university gown, until recently the sign of higher learning, witnesses to the same historical fact, for the gown proclaims its wearer a cleric. It was the long robe which marked the churchman off from the people in their short tunics. There is a long history behind my clerical outfitter's catalogue.

Towards the end of the last paragraph I used the word 'churchman' as though the clergy were the Church. It could seem so. Towards the end of the middle ages it was possible for Josse Clichtove to say 'ecclesia, quae in sacerdotibus constat . . .' as though the Church did consist of its priests. After all they performed its ceremonies and decided and taught its doctrines. They controlled its possessions, enjoyed its privileges and wore its insignia.

The practice was rather different from the theory. A strong

secular ruler kept a tight grip on ecclesiastical affairs. If his administrators were all clerics, what this really meant was that he used the revenues of the Church to maintain his civil service. Nevertheless, when I reflect on the status which the clergy had acquired, and the privileges which had accrued to them, my mind goes back to the seminary choirloft on those occasions when we were awaiting the arrival of the bishop. As in the wake of his many attendants he finally crossed the threshold in his magnificent raiment, a signal was given, so that we immediately greeted him with the resonant harmonies of 'Ecce Sacerdos Magnus'.

Chapter 5

THE BISHOP BELITTLED

By the early Middle Ages there was a very clear differentiation between cleric and layman. There was also a gulf between the higher and lower clergy. Every Latin presbyter might be entitled to wear a long gown, be taxed less and be urged to celibacy, but the lion's share of the power, prestige and wealth which had come to the Church since the time of Constantine, had gone to the higher ranks of the clergy. The relationship of bishop and presbyter had changed. In the days of Ignatius of Antioch, and for long after, there seems to have been one congregation in a city, with the bishop presiding over it and a presbyter sometimes deputising for him. The presbyter was very much the bishop's colleague, responsible with him for the general wellbeing of that little church, deputising at the eucharist occasionally, commonly reading and expounding the scriptures and leading in prayer.

The expansion of the Church meant that presbyters had to look after dependent churches in the city or even in the countryside. This greatly enhanced their ritual role. They were now presiding over their own services, rather than playing a subsidiary role at the side of the bishop. But they lost by the change. Separation from the bishop diminished their role as the bishop's colleagues in the administration of the church. As there was now a great deal more to manage, their loss was all the larger. This loss may have been in some ways the deacon's gain. The deacon had retained his personal connection with the bishop and was therefore at the centre of things. The Roman deacons are said to have been particularly powerful. Perhaps the presbyters became something of a clerical proletariat, while the bishops absorbed most of the profits of their business' expansion, and the deacons in the middle ranks of management did quite nicely for themselves. If so, time was preparing the presbyter's revenge. The diaconate would disappear or, to my mind more ignominiously, become a mere doorstep to be paused upon by those entering the portals of the presbyterate. And my lord bishop, for all his fine furbelows, was to find himself stripped of all theological justification — a nasty, if temporary, fate!

The stone which launched this cruel, if slowmoving, landslide was cast, not at the bishops, but at the deacons. The Ambrosiaster, a writer of the late fourth century, defends the presbyters against the pretensions of the Roman deacons on the grounds that the presbyters possess the same priesthood as the bishops. In St Paul, he maintains, bishop and presbyter mean the same thing. Some functions such as confirmation are normally reserved to the bishop, president of the presbyters, but the presbyter is in essence equally capable of performing them. St Jerome, a little later, was also aiming for the deacons when, like the Ambrosiaster, he claimed that bishop and presbyter stand on an equal footing sacerdotally, as both consecrate the body and blood of Christ. Presbyter and bishop differ in authority, not in priesthood. Here we have a distinction which was to wreak theological havoc. This is the dichotomy between what will later be termed *postestas ordinis* derived from the sacrament of orders, and *potestas jurisdictionis* which is attributed to some other source. The sacrament of orders is thought of as empowering a priest to perform certain actions, but not as conferring pastoral responsibility.

What we now refer to, rather inelegantly, as the 'ecclesial dimension' was lost to view. Bishops and presbyters were not seen as fulfilling complementary roles in the Church's work of salvation, but were measured against one another in terms of personal sacramental powers. What can this one do which this other one cannot? Eventually the answer was to look embarrassingly like 'Nothing'.

The 'ecclesial dimension' was plain enough to the Church of the Fathers. The Council of Chalcedon (451) forbade the practice of 'absolute' ordination, i.e. ordaining a priest or bishop without a definite congregation for which he was to care. This solicitude for the ecclesial dimension has left us an otherwise incomprehensible relic. Whenever a bishop is consecrated in order to assist another old, or simply over-worked, bishop, the new bishop is given a nominal see *in partibus infidelium*. A bishop cannot just be a bishop. He must be a bishop of somewhere. The sacramental powers should not be divorced from a full pastoral setting.

Unfortunately they often were. In the early monasteries a priest member sometimes fulfilled the community's liturgical requirements, while the monks looked to an unpriested abbot for pastoral care. In the same way, early Irish monasteries sometimes had a bishop among their number who ordained members to the priesthood, but the bishop was not the abbot, the leader of the community. This again dissociated the liturgical role from pastoral responsibility. So too did the employment of priests by feudal lords to perform the Mass and other ceremonies, but not to preach or exercise any pastoral supervision. We must remember also, that the separation of the local church under its own presbyter from the mother church under its bishop, put an end to the visible operation of collegiality. There was the priest in one place, and in the other his bishop, who reserved to himself certain sacramental functions and a general supervision.

We must now take a cursory look at the views of the mediaeval theologians. In the eleventh century Peter Damian, in the tradition of the Ambrosiaster and Jerome, says that episcopacy and presbyterate constitute one order because both have the highest conceivable power, the power to offer the body and blood of Christ. Here we have that obstinate focus on the Mass in total detachment from all the other work of the church. For Peter Damian the bishop has a higher *'dignitas'* and some ministries are reserved to him. In the following century Hugh of St Victor has the same approach. So does Peter Lombard, who was to set a permanent stamp on sacramental theology. For him the diaconate and presbyterate are sacramental, but the episcopate is a dignity and an office. Alexander of Hales in the thirteenth century defined the sacrament of orders as directed to the sacrament of communion. Since the episcopate is not so ordered, it is not a part of the sacrament of orders. It was the common opinion of many of the early scholastics that the episcopate is not a sacrament, but an office of jurisdiction. Some of them, like Gueric of St Quentin in the mid-thirteenth century, consider that a simple priest has the power to ordain other priests, but that the power ought to be exercised only by the bishop. St Thomas Aquinas accepted the view that the sacrament of orders should be defined in terms of the eucharist. He had at the same time an exalted concept of the episcopal office. He harmonised these two positions in the decision that ordination gave the priest power over the eucharistic body of Christ, while the bishop gave him power over the mystical body of Christ. For St Thomas, the 'principalitas' of the bishop over the mystical body of Christ is more than mere jurisdiction. For many of Thomas's successors it was not. For them the priest was the equal of the bishop in the sacramental order, but the bishop was superior in his power to ordain and confirm, the superiority being purely jurisdictional in origin.

The Protestant Reformation was to no small degree a reaction against the clericalism, the sacerdotalism of the Middle Ages. The Council of Trent in counter-reaction decisively affirmed the distinction between the ministerial priesthood and the priesthood of the faithful. It insisted on the power of the ordained priest to consecrate in the Mass and to forgive sins. Unfortunately the Council did not set these facts in the broader ecclesial context which might have reduced the mediaeval overemphasis on the minister's cultic role. In consequence, and very regrettably, a strongly sacerdotalist approach to the ministry was henceforth the hall-mark of Catholicism as against Protestantism. The Catholics had priests who were celibate and offered the sacrifice of the Mass; the Protestants had ministers, usually married, who 'took the service' and preached. Or so it seemed.

But in this chapter we are more concerned with the relationship of bishop and priest. Trent defined the doctrine that the episcopate, the presbyterate and the diaconate are of divine institution, and that the bishops are superior to the presbyters and can confirm and ordain and do other things which the priest cannot (*de Sacramento Ordinis*, cap. 4 and canons 6 and

7). But there is said nothing conclusive as to the source of the bishop's authority and his extra powers. The subject was d i s c u s s e d . Laynez, an i n f l u e n t i a l theologian, insisted trenchantly on the mediaeval distinction between the power of orders and the power of jurisdiction. He maintained that the bishop was a successor of the Apostles, only in the sense that he could consecrate other bishops, and asserted that their power of jurisdiction was derived from the Pope. Many a Tridentine theologian, including some future Popes, opposed Laynez, but Laynez was to win a postponed victory.

The post-Tridentine bishop was distinguished from the priest by his power to confirm, to ordain and by his general jurisdiction. However there was a general awareness that presbyters had in the past been empowered to confirm, and that in the East the priest was the ordinary minister of confirmation. Eventually in 1946, even in the Latin rite, the parish priest was delegated to confirm anyone in danger of death. The episcopal monopoly of the power to ordain presbyters seemed far more firmly based. Yet this plinth was not without its fissures. Leaving aside some patristic evidences and some obscure Carolingian precedents, there came to light in the third decade of this century authentic papal documents of the middle ages empowering presbyters (admittedly abbots) to ordain to the priesthood. The first, dated 1400, entitled the Abbot of St Osyth in Essex, to ordain his monks. In 1427 the Abbot of Altzelle in Saxony received the same concession. So, of the Bishop's peculiar powers we have left his unchallenged (so far as I know!) prerogative of consecrating other bishops. But that means little, so long as the episcopate itself means little.

Having lost so much sacramental ground to the presbyterate (All this was in the area of theory. I doubt if the theologians' persuasion that the presbyterate contained the radical power of confirmation and ordination did anything at all to redress the balance between a Cardinal of Paris and the miserable curés who served his poorer parishes, or between an Archbishop of Cologne and his obscurer pastors) the bishops were to lose ground on another front to the Papacy. The prestige of the Papacy mounted all through the nineteenth century and did NOT reach its climax in the First Vatican Council. In that Council a far from negligible minority opposed the definition of infallibility as inopportune, and the definition itself was very moderate. But the Ultramontanes used their limited victory as a springboard for further claims. It became the common teaching of theologians, if we stretch that honourable title to cover the compilers of theological manuals, that the jurisdiction of bishops is derived from the Holy See. This seems to be the view enshrined in the Encyclical *Mystici Corporis* (June 1943) (Dz 2287). Laynez' view had come to be the cornerstone of an edifice, in the design of which the episcopate seemed hardly to figure.

On such grounds could my own lecturer on the sacraments describe a priest as a suppressed bishop. So the soberly garbed gentlemen at the front of my clerical outfitter's catalogue, only needed a missive from Rome to release their power to confirm and ordain, to give them jurisdiction over a diocese, and turn them into the colourful silk clad figures at the back of the catalogue.

Chapter 6

VATICAN II. THE EPISCOPATE VINDICATED

In 1953 I sat in the seminary lecture room, as our instructor in the theology of orders explained that he saw himself as a 'suppressed bishop'. In 1963 I sat in a presbytery dining room, an audience of one, while the parish priest expressed his misgivings about the Second Vatican Council. 'This council', he said 'will increase the power of the bishops, and will raise the status of the laity — and we shall be in between.' His language was untechnical, but his judgement astute. The situation he predicted with the priest squeezed to a thinness between bishop and layman, is literally verified in the dogmatic constitution *Lumen Gentium.* In that most characteristic and significant document, Chapter Three deals with the hierarchical structure of the Church. It has section after orotund section proclaiming the fulness of the episcopal mission and the glory thereof. At the end of the chapter, hanging there like a skimpy tail on a robust elephant, is one flat section which deals with both priesthood and diaconate. The diaconate, which has been dead for centuries in the Western Church, has almost as much space as the priesthood. But the laity has the whole of Chapter Four to itself. Manning had written, 'There can be conceived no office higher, and no power greater than the office of the priest'. But in Vatican II that office is sandwiched between the sublime role of the episcopate and the lofty vocation of the Christian layman.

The Council Fathers did not deliberately set out to contradict Cardinal Manning, or the mediaeval theologians, or the neo-scholastic manuals of the nineteenth century. The Council spoke in an entirely different fashion because they approached the question from an entirely different angle. The mediaeval scholastics with Jerome before them and a stream of theologians after them, investigated the bishop and scrutinised the priest, by focussing upon their office in isolation, and asking, 'What can this man do which is distinctive?' The Second

43

Vatican Council looked first and long at the whole Church, its nature and its mission, and then tried to express the role of the ministry and the laity within that context.

This shift of perspective is extremely important. It seemed to come with disconcerting abruptness. In fact it had long been waiting in the wings to make an overdue appearance in the centre of the stage. At the Council of Trent a number of theologians had discussed the role of the bishop in terms of his relationship to the whole Church. The future Innocent IX, then Bishop of Nicasto, spoke of episcopal consecration as the contraction of an indissoluble marriage between the bishop and the whole Church, while the future Urban VII claimed that the bishops were the successors of the Apostles in their ministry towards the entire Church. Similar views were expressed by other important members of the Council.

Nor did the sense of the entire Church as the proper context in which to gauge the nature of the episcopate, wither away in the centuries after Trent. In the mid-seventeenth century the canonist Riciullo said that consecration renders a man a bishop *per totam ecclesiam*. Other canonists of the same period but from different countries, agreed with him. Writers in the eighteenth century continued to uphold the universal, collegial aspect of the episcopal office. The Benedictine, Gerbert, taught it explicitly. So did his contemporary, the Dominican Christianopoulos, and in 1789 the Jesuit Bolgeni, published a developed ecclesiology which seems to anticipate Vatican II.

But a sense of the whole Church requires more than an awareness of the collegial role of the bishop. The authentic, ecclesial vision is more comprehensive than that. It is a perception of the Church as one interrelated whole, none of whose parts is wholly passive, none of whose parts is understandable except in relation to the rest. This conception of the Church preoccupied many Catholic, Lutheran and Anglican theologians in the late eighteenth and nineteenth centuries. Among Catholics the chief place must go to Möhler of Tubingen, who in 1828 published *Die Einheit Der Kirche*. Möhler emphasised the Pauline doctrine that the totality of the gifts of the Spirit is given only to the totality of believers, and that the touchstone of each charism is its aptitude to combine with the gifts of other members of the community. The theologian depends on the common experience of the community — and the community depends on him to illuminate its shared faith. The ascetic cannot exist without his fellow Christians in the world, while they need the inspiration of his idealistic witness. Authority is an organ within the organism, not something controlling it from outside. Authority presupposes the activities of others, which it coordinates.

Cardinal Newman, whose writings are scattered roughly over the half century following the publication of *Die Einheit*, appears to have come quite independently to the same conclusions. He taught that grace is social and ecclesial, that teaching authority in the Church is not oracular, but 'a charism of discrimination'. Newman's ecclesiology is not to be found in any one work equivalent to Möhler's masterpiece, but it has been well urged that his 'Idea Of A University' should be read as an analogue of his ideal of the Church. So when he asserts that it is the entire university community that educates the member, he is also saying that it is the whole church which instructs and sanctifies the individual Christian.

Some of the above may not seem highly relevant to Vatican II's doctrine of the ministry. I must insist that it is. Because the ministry plays a key role in the Church it will be interpreted variously, according as the Church is conceived of differently. The Council's view of the ministry springs directly from its way of thinking of the Church, and that is very much in the tradition of Möhler and Newman.

It is also important for those of us who grew up before Vatican II to understand why that vision of the Church as an organic community, which the nineteenth century had achieved, was, as I said, kept waiting in the wings until the mid-twentieth century. It was crowded off the stage partly by the neo-scholastic revival, and partly by heavy stress on Papal authority. But I am convinced that we must look further afield and think of the general climate of the nineteenth century. In

Western Europe this was a time of centralisation, of standardisation, of vigorous administration. The states of Germany
were fused into the new German Empire, the states of Italy
merged into one Kingdom. European governments adopted
wholly new standards of responsibility and efficiency. They
trained and equipped huge armies; developed competent
bureaucracies, instituted national systems of education and
promoted the building of roads, railways and telegraph
systems. In this century Western Europe extended its power in
Asia, and took over most of Africa and Oceania. In these
regions also, Europeans administered, standardised, educated
and built. Bengalis, the Bantu and Samoans were taught
English. Moroccans, Senegalese and Vietnamese learned
French. The affairs of Africans, Asians and Pacific Islanders
were ultimately decided in the capitals of Europe. It is true
that the nineteenth century was partial to democracy with
elections and wide, perhaps universal, manhood suffrage. But
even if they had a vote in an occasional election, people were
being administered, legislated for, conscripted, taught and
generally managed as never before.

The Church of the nineteenth century fitted into this scene.
It had the nineteenth century energy. Pious organisations
flourished; the older religious orders expanded, many new
ones were created. The missionary effort was heroic. And
there was a corresponding movement of intensified centralisation in Rome and an increasing standardisation e.g. in
liturgy and canon law. Eskimos, Congolese and Polynesians
were baptised with Latin formulae, and instructed in the piety
of contemporary Latin Catholicism. Small wonder that most
churchmen thought in terms of rulers and ruled ('In the
Church there is no House of Commons', said Cardinal Manning
to a group of distinguished laymen), in terms of teachers and
taught. ('I am the only teacher in this diocese', declared an
English bishop, who still survives. At first his audience thought
that he was joking.) It is not surprising that in such a climate
the Möhler-Newman perception that the Spirit moves in the
whole people, that orthodoxy is preserved in the whole body
of the Church, that it is the whole body of the Church which

educates, seeped through with such difficulty. Nor did the totalitarian movements of the twentieth century help.

Rather one has to explain why the Möhler-Newman vision ever prevailed. I think that the explanation is to be found in the combined effects of the liturgical movement, the increased study of patristic writings and the more intensive study of the scriptures. These forces had by 1962 greatly modified the outlook of theologians. Consequently the Second Vatican Council did not use the approach of the scholastic theologians. They did not ask, 'What can a bishop do which a priest cannot? What can a priest do which a layman cannot?' Their most important statements are set in a full ecclesial context. The great document of the Council is *Lumen Gentium* on the Church. This begins with a chapter on the 'Mystery of the Church'. The second chapter is on 'The People of God'. Only in the third chapter are we introduced to the hierarchical structure of the Church. There are twelve sections in this particular chapter. In ten of them the lofty patristic conception of the episcopal office is resoundingly and irreversibly vindicated. The bishops are 'the successors of the Apostles, who together with the successor of St Peter, the visible Head of the whole Church, govern the house of the living God' (sec. 18). They are 'teachers of doctrine, priests (*sacerdotes*) of sacred worship and officers of good order' (*gubernationis ministri*). 'They have taken up the service of the community with their helpers, the priests and deacons' (sec. 20). As the Council, with some exceptions, uses *sacerdos* in the cultic contexts and *presbyter* in others, I have decided to depart from the commonly used English translation of the Council documents in this one point, and use 'presbyter' where the Latin text does so.

So it is in section 20 that we have the first mention of the presbyter. It is as the bishop's helper in the service of the community. Section 21 repeats the point: 'In the bishops, therefore, for whom presbyters are assistants, Our Lord, Jesus Christ, is present in the midst of those who believe.' Seven more sections describe the episcopal office. 'The order of bishops is the successor to the college of the apostles in teaching authority and pastoral rule, or rather, in the episcopal order the apostolic body continues without a break' (sec. 21). In the first place the bishop is dealt with as a member of an order, of a 'college' with responsibility for the whole Church. When the duties of the bishop are set out, the first to be considered is 'the preaching of the gospel' (sec. 25). The bishop is next considered as 'the steward of the grace of the supreme priesthood' (sec. 26), sanctifying the faithful 'through the sacraments, the fruitful distribution of which they direct'. And 'Finally by the example of their manner of life they must be an influence for good.' Thirdly (27) comes the government of a particular diocese. 'This power . . . is proper, ordinary and immediate . . . nor are they to be regarded as vicars of the Roman Pontiff for they exercise an authority which is proper to them.'

Of the twelve sections of the chapter on the 'Hierarchical Structure of the Church' ten have gone to the eloquent exposition of the episcopal office. Of the remaining two, one goes to the presbyters and the last to the diaconate, which as a permanent office had ceased to exist. The section says that it can be restored 'where it is opportune'. Chapter IV with its nine sections is concerned with 'The Laity'. It would, of course, be naif to compute the importance which the Council attaches to a subject by the number of sections which they give to it. Yet to deal with the presbyterate more or less as an appendange to the episcopate in little more space than that given to the defunct, if resurrectable, diaconate is very much to put the presbyter 'in his place'.

After this another Jerome, another Gueric of St Quentin, is hardly likely to suggest a basic equality of bishop and presbyter. At the same time, without attempting to pick up the splintered cudgels of Jerome and Gueric, I would presume to suggest that the Council deals with this relationship in a highly theoretical way. The bishop may be an 'authentic teacher' (25), but the majority of his flock will rarely hear his voice, as it is the presbyters who actually expound the gospel and the bishop's pastorals. The bishop may be the 'steward of the grace of the supreme priesthood', but it is a presbyter who

48

presides when the bulk of people hear Mass, a presbyter who baptizes, shrives, anneals and buries them. Of course, preaching and the administration of the sacraments are controlled by the bishop. Certainly he administers the diocese. But he is a faraway figure to most of his people. 'What does a bishop do with himself?', I was asked by a sixthformer who was a daily Mass-goer. 'The bishop does nothing for me', said one very devout and theologically competent young teacher. Perhaps the Council should have added a section advising the bishop to have a good P.R.O.

When it is the presbyters who *de facto* do most of the preaching and the administering of the sacraments, and who implement the bishop's policy, their treatment in this historic document seems less than adequate. But short though section 28 may be, it holds a moderate amount of matter. It begins by saying that 'the bishops have legitimately handed on to different individuals in the Church various degrees of participation in the ministry'. If this were meant to be an historical statement that the apostles erected the episcopacy, and that the bishops then decided to share this mission with others, then it would simply be untrue. Development in the Apostolic and post-Apostolic Age was, as I have shown in earlier chapters, a great deal more complex than that. To make one obvious point, the Apostles were themselves assisted by 'elders' in their own lifetime, whereas the full episcopal mission could only mature after their deaths. There was some sort of 'presbyteral' participation in the ministry before there was a developed episcopal one. The Council's statement must not be read as a literal description of historical events, but rather as a picture of the eventual relationship of bishop and prebyter. The section goes on: 'although presbyters do not possess the highest degree of the priesthood . . . they are nevertheless united with the bishop in sacerdotal dignity.' 'They are consecrated to preach the gospel, shepherd the faithful, and celebrate divine worship as true priests of the New Testament.' It is interesting that the cultic function, which for most people defines the priest, comes last on the list. But the expansion of these duties is taken in the reverse order, and it is the Mass which is treated at greatest length and with greatest eloquence. This strikes me as a clever arrangement. It connects the over focusing of the past upon the presbyter's cultic role, and yet does not derogate from the incomparable dignity of the Mass.

The ecclesial dimension of the presbyter's work is heavily underscored. The presbyters make the bishop 'present in a certain sense in the individual local congregations'. Presumably because their bishop is a member of the episcopal college, the presbyters 'make the universal church visible in their own locality'. This consciousness of the whole Church and the whole diocese and the universal Church should not remain a solemn thought; it should lead them 'to lend their effort to the pastoral work of the whole diocese and even of the entire church'.

Part of the ecclesial dimension of the presbyterate should be the close relationship of bishop and presbyter, the 'intimate brotherhood' of his presbyters among themselves, the unity the presbyter should produce in his congregation and the zeal he should have for the unity of the human race. Here we have not merely an ecclesial context as the setting of the priest's mission, but a context as wide as humanity. The breadth of Möhler's and Newman's vision has at this point been surpassed!

Chapter 7

CONCILIAR CONSIDERATION CONTINUED

In the great document on the Church the presbyters, as we have seen, rated a single section. But there is an entire decree on the 'Ministry and Life of Priests' (Presbyters?). There is also a Decree on the Bishop's Pastoral Office in which the presbyters are inevitably involved. Let us take the second document first. In this decree the presbyters are three times labelled 'prudent co-operators of the bishop' (*providi co-operatores*) (sections 15, 28, 34). This phrase which occurred in *Lumen Gentium* becomes something of an incantation in the Council documents, reminding one of such literary parallels as 'milk-white hands' and the 'wine-dark sea'. The Council certainly drives home the point that a presbyter is to work with the bishop. There is some insistence on interdependence; the bishop should discuss matters with the presbyters, presbyters should be united among themselves and think in terms of the whole diocese (section 28). The heavy emphasis on the presbyter being the bishop's helper is slightly redressed by the phrase 'shepherds in their own right' (sect. 30). The stress is on the pastoral work of the presbyter, of which his liturgical activity is part and yet also the centre. The celebration of Mass should be 'the centre and culmination of the whole life of the Christian community'. Again there is emphasis on the whole parish, on the parish feeling itself to be part of the whole diocese and of the whole Church.

This decree takes cognisance of the distinction between the diocesan clergy and the religious priests (*sacerdotes*, section 34). If ordained presbyters, the religious are also '*providi co-operatores*' of the episcopal order. The Council tries to reconcile their cooperation in the work of the diocese under the direction of the bishop with the preservation of their distinctive spirit and the cohesion of their own congregation.

The decree seems to me to tackle this matter on a practical rather than a theoretical basis. The point is important. At times the Council seems to have a very simple ecclesiology. It almost seems to say that the ministry of the Church is the work of the bishops, but as the bishop cannot be everywhere doing everything, he has some presbyters to help. Such an approach cannot cope theoretically with the religious orders. Usually their members are not, except temporarily, members of the diocese. They have their own superiors, national and international; they have their own distinctive ideals and aims. In certain respects they do not look to the bishop for leadership. The Superior General of a religious order is an intriguing special case of the presbyter. He may be responsible for deploying the abilities of several thousand presbyters, far more than a bishop normally disposes of. But sacramentally the Superior General is a presbyter. Yet he is more directly concerned to think in terms of the universal church than is the bishop administering a diocese, and it seems appropriate that he should attend General Councils, as he may well do.

But we have by no means finished with the run-of-the-mill variety of presbyter. The Second Vatican Council issued a 'Decree on the Ministry and Life of Priests' (Presbyters, rather!). I must try to avoid compiling a synopsis of this document and select only those passages which deal with the nature of the priesthood. There is a declaration in the preface: 'By sacred ordination and by the mission they receive from their bishops, priests are promoted to the service of Christ, the Teacher, the Priest and the King. They share in His ministry of unceasingly building up the Church on earth into the People of God, the Body of Christ and the Temple of the Holy Spirit'. Then, interestingly, the document speaks of the priesthood of the whole body of the faithful: 'all the faithful are made a holy and royal priesthood' (2). But there is diversity: 'the same Lord established certain ministers among the faithful in order to join them together in one body'. 'These ministers would be able to offer sacrifice and remit sins'. Here the document cleverly juxtaposes the ecclesial and cultic aspects of the ministry. Then we return to the Apostolic mission and, of course, the bishops. 'Through these same Apostles He made their successors, the bishops, sharers in His consecration and

His mission. Their ministerial role has been handed down to presbyters in a limited degree . . . they are co-workers [not this time 'prudent'] of the episcopal order.' Next is mentioned the sacrament of Orders: 'the sacerdotal office of the presbyter is conferred by that special sacrament through which priests. . . are marked with a special character and are so configured to Christ the Priest that they can act in the Person of Christ the Head'. The presbyter must first 'shoulder the sacred task of the gospel . . . through the apostolic proclamation of the gospel the People of God is called together and assembled'. This people can then offer itself 'a sacrifice . . . pleasing to God'. Through the presbyter this sacrifice is united with that of Christ. Here the evangelical work of the ministry has been put into sacrificial, sacerdotal language, which leads neatly into the mention of the Eucharist. There follows a passage which deserves unabridged quotation. 'The purpose, therefore, which presbyters pursue by their ministry and life, is the glory of God the Father as it is to be achieved in Christ. That glory consists in this: that men knowingly, freely and gratefully accept what God has achieved through Christ and manifest it in their whole lives.' Whenever I read that passage I am moved to all sorts of good resolutions.

Section three, without solving the practical problems it raises, expounds the two sidedness of the ministry. 'Priests are taken from among men and appointed for men. . . Hence they deal with other men as brothers.' They are 'set apart . . . but not that they may be separated.' 'Their ministry . . . forbids them to be conformed to this world. Yet at the same time this ministry requires that they live in this world among men.' In the fourth section it is laid down that the primary duty of the presbyter is the 'proclamation of the gospel of God to all'. Section five deals with the sacraments and recalls St Ignatius' teaching that in their administration the presbyter is linked with the bishop. 'Thus in a certain way, they make him present in every gathering of the faithful.' The section also points out that the Eucharist is 'the source and apex of the whole work of preaching the gospel.' The section weaves together very impressively the use of the sacraments, the practice of prayer and the Christian conduct of life on the part of the people, and the presbyter's part in producing the same seamless texture. Section six introduces the word 'authority', but the leadership it describes is that of 'educators in the faith'. Its aim is 'that the faithful must be led 'to the development of their own vocation . . . and to that freedom with which Christ has made us free'. The note of community, local and universal, is sounded as clearly and as powerfully as in the other documents. 'The office of pastor is not confined to the care of the faithful as individuals, but it is also extended to the formation of a genuine Christian community . . . it must embrace not only the local Church, but the universal Church. . . . It should also prepare the way to Christ for all men'. In Section seven, which deals with the practical relationship of presbyter to bishop, the bishop is told to regard the presbyters as 'necessary helpers and counsellors' and as 'brothers and friends'. I rather like that. It goes a little way beyond *providi co-operatores*. I am glad to hear the Council admit that we are actually needed!

But even after the Council has dubbed me a 'counsellor', to be received as a friend or brother, I do not feel emboldened to offer the bishop much advice, and certainly not with the frankness of a friend or relation. Perhaps anticipating my diffidence the Council decrees that there should be set up some form of senate of priests 'to give effective assistance to the bishop in his government of the diocese'. 'The union of presbyters with their bishop is all the more necessary' . . . because . . . 'no presbyter can in isolation or singlehandedly accomplish his mission in a satisfactory way'.

Developing that last point Section eight states that the presbyters of a diocese form one 'presbytery' carrying on one ministry, no matter what their actual assignment. Section nine deals briefly with the relationship to the laity to whom they are 'father and teacher'. They must 'promote the dignity of the laity', 'honour that just freedom which is due to everyone', 'recognise their experience and competence' and foster 'the various humble and exalted charisms of the laity'. The obligations of the presbyter reach out to include the lapsed, the separated Christians and the unbelievers. This point is expressed again in Section ten: 'every priestly ministry shares in the universality of the mission entrusted by Christ to his apostles'. There are a further twelve sections dealing with the life of the presbyter, but they are not really concerned with the fundamental nature of the ministry.

When I wish to sum up for myself the teaching of Vatican II on the subject of the priesthood, I do so by comparing it with Cardinal Manning's *Eternal Priesthood*. Manning published that work in 1883. Its twentieth edition came out in 1931. The work was still being warmly praised in 1951. The Cardinal says that the Apostles were ordained at the Last Supper, and received the power of absolution three days later. 'In these two powers the priesthood was complete. The pastoral authority and the world-wide commission of the Apostles were not yet given'. Vatican II reverses this. The Council begins with the Church, proceeds to the responsibilities of the Apostles within and for the Church, the transmission of that responsibility to the episcopate, and the presbyters' subordinate share in that responsibility. Cardinal Manning in the scholastic tradition defines the priesthood by its powers: 'the twofold jurisdiction over His natural body and over the mystical body'. The Council does not define in terms of power, but of responsibility. It teaches that the priest, as the bishop's co-worker, must preach the gospel, administer the sacraments and 'gather God's family together as a brotherhood of living unity, and lead it through Christ and in the Spirit to God the Father' (*The Ministry and Life of Presbyters*, section 6.), a triple task which finds its culmination and recapitulation in the Eucharist. In Manning's work there are two real persons, the priest and his Divine Master. The laity, fellow priests, ecclesiastical superiors are, of course, mentioned, but they are shadowy, peripheral figures in a world which is centred upon the priest. For the Council it is the context which gives significance. The office of presbyter draws its meaning from the Church of which he is a minister, the episcopate which he assists, the diocesan presbyterate to which he belongs, the community which he serves, the world which he must help to save. Manning stresses the priest's isolation. The priest is 'never more alone than when he is in thronging streets and crowded rooms'. The Council constantly emphasises the note of community, that the priest's existence is one of participation.

Chapter 8

PROBLEMS RESOLVED, UNSOLVED
AND PARTLY SOLVED

Almost two decades ago I had a very interesting conversation with a young Syrian Jesuit. He told me that everybody took it for granted that he was a convert from Islam, whereas his district in Syria had been Christian since just after the time of the Apostles. The Moslem conquest had not destroyed Christian belief or practice in the area, but had isolated it, and so preserved its very ancient forms. He was particularly interesting on the subject of the priesthood. He told me that when the village priest died, the villagers looked round and chose someone whom they respected as a good Christian man, and whom they knew would be acceptable to the village as a whole, and then despatched him to the bishop. The bishop would keep the man with him for three months or so, to satisfy himself about the man's character and disposition and his knowledge of the ceremonies. This last could normally be presumed, as the villagers were usually as familiar with their vernacular liturgy as the celebrating priest. If satisfied on these counts, the bishop would, after some further instruction and good advice, ordain the man and send him back to his village to carry out the duties of a priest. The new priest would not be a young man. The village expected maturity. He would naturally be a married man, who had lived among his neighbours, wholly one of them in upbringing and daily life.

How very different from our Western stereotype of the priest with his years of seminary training, which may have begun in boyhood, reared in, living in, perhaps engrossed in a distinct, professional, clerical world! My language may seem a little loaded in favour of the Syrian pastor because it is always easy to be starry-eyed about a situation one has never seen working.

Which is the right formula? Or, more eirenically, which is the preferable one? A conservative Catholic of the West might say that he wants his pastor to be distinctive in life, and dress, because his work is concerned with an eternal, supramundane order. Further, the exiguous training of the Syrian parish priest, which can hardly have raised him above the theological competence of his congregation, would seem to us pitifully inadequate. The interesting thing here is that the Western conservative, as so often, in supporting what he is used to, is upholding what is comparatively new. The Syrian pastor represents a far older Christian tradition than does our celibate, seminary product. That does not mean that we should be better Christians if we cashiered our professional clergy, and ordained the President of the S.V.P. or the Supreme Knight of the K.S.C. 'In the early Church they used to . . . ' is an argument of limited force. It is not unthinkable that we might have improved on the practices of the early Christians, or at least made some sensible adaptations to changing circumstances. But the usages of the early Church, and obscure survivals thereof, show us that what we have grown used to in the West in recent centuries is not the only valid Catholic way of doing things.

I have shot from Vatican II to a remote Syrian village largely for a change of scene. I also wanted to raise a question about the ministry, the vague, general question of 'life style', as an example of a problem to which there is no simple, final answer in the documents of Vatican II. There are many such problems, and this should not surprise us. A General Council, even after intense preparation and long discussions does not normally exhaust a subject, leaving no matter for further discussion.

One matter the Council did settle. It made it irreversibly clear that there is a difference, a great difference, between the bishop and the presbyter. But whether they have done the presbyter anything like full justice, seems to me very doubtful. The disintegration of the theology of the episcopate, which I chronicled in Chapter V, required urgent attention. It certainly got it. But correction easily becomes over-correction. The searchlight of conciliar eloquence was played long and lovingly on the responsibility and dignity of the episcopate leaving the presbyterate largely in an obscurity penetrated only by gleams reflected from the splendour of those who inherit the apostolic mission. Very often, as I have pointed out, the presbyter seems little better than a useful tool of the bishop, an instrument through which the bishop can regularly reach his flock, as though the presbyterate existed solely to cope with the problem of numbers, space and time. The Council is not always so belittling. I have pointed out that the presbyters are called 'necessary helpers' and even 'shepherds in their own right'. But these are only very sketchy indications, rather than the clear outlines of a theology which would treat the presbyterate as a major organ in the living body of the Church, and not as some providential accessory.

The Council has not done justice to the fact that there was some sort of presbyteral participation in the apostolic mission before the office of bishop as successor to the Apostles was required. They have passed over in very academic fashion the actual situation in which it is the presbyters who actually supply most of the sacraments, who preach and instruct and are the focus of parish life, which is much more real to people than diocesan life. In practice it is the presbyterate who cope with the overwhelming mass of the work of the ministry. Would we refer to the teaching profession as 'prudent cooperators' of the Ministry of Education, or describe the coalminers as 'necessary helpers' of the Coal Board? I have already commented on how awkwardly the bishop-centred theories of the Council fit, or fail to fit, the presbyters who belong to religious orders and congregations, and these are too numerous and play too large a part in the ministry for the difficulty to be ignored.

In general, the Council would seem to have paid insufficient attention to the complementarity of bishop and presbyter, to the fact that one role calls for the other. The activities of a priest attempting to act in total independence would be partly meaningless because he exists to link people with the episcopate, and through them with the rest of the Church. But how much meaning is there in a bishop without a presbyterate? It would be possible to consecrate a bishop and send him unsupported into missionary territory, but would it not seem like sending an admiral to sea in a one man submarine? Vatican II defines a presbyter in terms of his relationship to the episcopate; but perhaps the episcopate does not make a lot of sense without the presbyterate.

Besides establishing a very firm, if not totally satisfactory, distinction between the bishop and presbyter, the Second Vatical Council took another very definite step. While I was working on the first chapters of this book I heard a priest say, rather disconcertingly after Vatican II, 'I cannot see how we can possibly recognise the orders of other denominations unless they accept the sacrifice of the Mass'. For this particular priest, a priest is someone who offers sacrifice. This is, or has been, a very common notion. I once remarked that I had been ordained to preach. My then superior corrected me. He said that I had been ordained to offer sacrifice. According to this school of thought, the pagan priest, and the Jewish priest offered sacrifice, and the Christian priest offers the greatest sacrifice of all. This is an agreeably simple, coherent view with an univocal concept of priesthood-in-general applying neatly to the pagan, Jewish and Christian priest and even to the High Priest of the Exillions whom I watched with fraternal interest this evening on 'Dr Who'. But it ignores too many facts. It ignores the fact that for some hundreds of years the Christians never used of their own ministers the term which they used for the Greek and Jewish sacrifice-offerers. It ignores the fact that our word 'priest' comes from '*presbyteros*', an 'elder', a term which has no connection with the Temple or sacrifice. The first generations of Christians did not think of their religious leaders as fitting neatly into the same category as the pagan and Jewish cult officials. It is most unfortunate that their successors were not equally clear on the matter.

The Second Vatical Council should have made the continuance of that particular error impossible, but as yet there seem to be many priests who think of themselves primarily, even essentially, as Mass-sayers — with or without a congregation. The Council always treats the ministry as threefold. Thus the Decree *On Priestly Formation* which I have not previously quoted says that the training of the seminarist ought to provide for his development 'after the model of Our Lord, Jesus Christ, who was Teacher, Priest and Shepherd'. The students should 'be readied (*sic*) for the ministry of the word', 'the ministry of worship and sanctification' and 'the ministry of the shepherd' (4). This is the common division and the common order in all the relevant documents. In *Lumen Gentium* the bishops are teachers of doctrine, priests of sacred worship and officers of good order (20). In the *Decree on the Bishops' Pastoral Office* the phrasing is different, but the division and order exactly the same, 'the duty of teaching' (12 & 13), the 'duty to sanctify' (15) and 'the office of father and pastor' (16). The *Decree on the Ministry and Life of Priests* (Presbyters!) keeps the same triple division of the presbyter's ministry and the same order. The Council did not in any way 'downgrade' the Mass. They enhanced its importance by showing plainly how it answers to all three aspects of the ministry, because it teaches, sanctifies and brings the community together under the presidency of the pastor, and this is a much broader, much richer concept of the Mass than the performance of a sacrificial act.

We have seen how St Jerome, by focusing narrowly on the priest's power to offer Mass confused the whole relationship of bishop and presbyter for one and a half thousand years, a remarkable, if unfortunate, achievement. The same straitened and therefore distorting concept of the priesthood has, ever since the Reformation, obstructed the Catholic's view of the ministry of the Reformed Churches. If a priest is essentially the offerer of sacrifice, and the reformed churches did not accept the Tridentine definition of the sacrifice of the Mass, then they obviously have no priesthood. And if the Christian ministry is pre-eminently priestly, then the Reformed have no ministry worth taking seriously. Thus it was quite logical for a Roman Catholic bishop in 1950 (I may be one year out) to object to an Anglican bishop blessing an ecumenical gathering. The Catholics present, maintained the bishop, would prefer not to be blessed by someone whom they must regard as a layman. Much less logical, and even less charitable, was the vituperation of a certain northern priest when he described the Bishop of Durham as 'a layman living in concubinage'.

The Council's revivification of the fuller view of the ministry sets ministers of the reformed churches in a different and far kindlier light. As a Protestant minister preaches the word and assembles and leads a congregation to which he tenders the sacraments and over whom he presides liturgically, the differences between him and the Catholic presbyter as described by Vatican II, though not minor, are certainly partial. Because the eucharistic liturgy is central to the ministry, as long as denominations differ about the first, their views of the second will not correspond precisely; but there can be a great deal of overlap. Conversely, when the Anglican-Roman Catholic International Commission had arrived at a 'substantial agreement' on the doctrine of the Eucharist, then within two years they were able to reach an agreed statement on 'Ministry and Ordination'.

The considerable rapprochement, even harmonisation, of Roman Catholic and Anglican views does not entail the immediate, or even imminent, reciprocal recognition of one another's orders. It is one thing to agree about the nature of the ministry and even the transmission of orders, and quite another to concur about the facts of transmission in any particular case or set of cases. But certainly the Council, by presenting the ministry in its triple pastoral deployment, allows us to examine the old question of the orders of the reformed Churches in a different and much kindlier light.

Now let me return to that intriguing High Priest of the Exillions and his colleagues. Their preparations, frustrated of course, to sacrifice the Doctor and his young female colleague, took place in a pillared hall amidst an intense, impersonal chanting. Religion, you see, is made recognisable by its distinctive architecture, distinctive music and peculiar functionaries. The creators of 'Dr Who' know that the public has a notion of 'priesthood-in-general' vaguely applicable to all religions, Christian, pagan or space-fictional.

It seems a great pity that Christians have accepted such a generic concept of priesthood since it reduces the distinctiveness of Christianity. But should we harp on the uniqueness of Christianity? To demand that the organisation of the Christian Church should have nothing in common with other religious organisations, smacks of total contempt for those others, and might well produce a form of organisation so exotic as to be inhuman. Christianity has a unique revelation: yet its mission is to all men. The first fact will incline the Church to emphasise and guard its distinctiveness; the second will incline it to use categories with which the rest of the world is familiar, which human beings have found widely acceptable. The first generation of Christians presumably wanted to stress the difference between their ministers and the Jewish and pagan cult officials. Later generations perceived the similarities and saw some advantage in using a common vocabulary. I think that we should not be too censorious about that decision. We should also feel free to reverse it.

Nor, I suspect, should we be too censorious about a parallel and slightly earlier decision, the one to accept in the Roman Empire the civic status which the pagan cult-officials enjoyed. Some of our modern religious radicals seem to urge that we should ecstatically embrace the secular world, and simultaneously shun all its structures. This, for me, makes no sort of sense. The Christian ministry may have been right, I only say 'may', to accept integration into the social structure of the Roman Empire. It is possible that the advantages outweighed the disadvantages, or seemed to. One now clear disadvantage was the contamination of the gospel idea of authority as humble service, with quite unchristian notions of domination and prestige. It was undoubtedly a mistake to allow this adulteration of a key Christian concept with Roman and feudal practices. But the mistake has been compounded by a worse one. When Christians adopt something from the contemporary secular world, a language, a symbol, a system, be what it may, then that thing, because it is used by the Church, acquires a largely spurious sacredness of its own. It becomes a part of Catholicism and we feel obliged to cling to it when the rest of the world has dropped it.

Twenty five years ago I asked an American student if

Protestant America was not repelled by the titles, garments and other would-be-aristocratic trappings of the Catholic hierarchy. With the intransigence of the Boston Irish he replied 'We don't care what the Protestants think'. In the Roman world the Church naturally spoke Latin, and Latin became a sacred language. The ministers in Roman times wore Roman clothes and today I have to say Mass in much the same sort of garb, because they are now sacred vestments. A Catholic bishop has a coat of arms, is in many countries called 'my Lord' and commonly lives and moves in some state. What was a regrettable aspect of his assimilation to the Roman official and later the feudal lord has become almost inseparable from the exercise of ecclesiastical responsibilities. Hence in the republican, egalitarian USA, one cardinal felt it proper to build a throneroom in which to hold audiences, and another felt obliged to refuse all invitations which did not guarantee him his full precedence as a 'prince of the Church'.

But let us descend to the humbler stratum of the 'inferior clergy'. As feudalism disappeared the bulk of the clergy found themselves located socially among the expanding professional classes, the people with above-average education and some 'responsibility'. Again I should be slow to censure our predecessors for this. This status came to them, rather than was sought by them. Even now I wonder how much option we have. Presumably we want our clerics to have a good education and professional training, while responsibility is quite inevitable. If those things carry status, can status be wholly waived?

In one matter we do have an option and I would urge we use it decisively. We should make as clean a break as we can with 'priesthood-in-general', and shake off as many associations as we can with the ox-slayers of the past. The Council has made it clear enough that the Christian minister is not to think of himself as primarily a performer of rites. He is a minister of the word, a liturgical president and the guide of his community. For a long time we have concentrated on the priest as Mass-sayer in quite a disproportionate way, and one effect of this imbalance has been to reinforce the resemblance to the cow-carving hierophants of yore. We have a great deal to do to redress the balance. We must insist very much less on the cultic role of this minister, and make much more of his function as teacher and guide.

Because the word 'priest' has come to be a generic term for the cultic official of any religion, even in space fantasy, I suggest that we should do well to drop the term completely. Perhaps we could call ourselves 'presbyters', which is the original form of the word, which is still in canonical use, and which is entirely unassociated with Temples, blood-letting and the scrutinising of entrails. For the Christians of the late Roman Empire there may have been some point in permitting these associations. But there is no advantage to us, and the grave disadvantage, that these associations cloud our understanding of the Christian ministry. It is a real distortion to define the Christian minister in terms of temple and sacrifice, and when Vatican II has described the ministry in the broader context of word, liturgy and community, we should do all we can to shake off the narrow and obfuscatory notion of ourselves as essentially cult-performers.

Much of our clerical 'style' would seem to derive from the priest's being seen and seeing himself as an hieratic functionary, and also from the fact that our predecessors had their place in the ranked, graded society of the late Roman Empire and the Middle Ages. So we are called 'Reverend Father' or some such equivalent, and dress differently. The 'distinctness' of the priest is further reinforced by the effect of the almost monastic atmosphere of the seminary, and by celibacy. The difference between himself and the general public is increased unavoidably by his work. When the busiest part of your year comes at the holiday seasons of Christmas and Easter, when the busiest part of your week is the weekend and Monday your best day for relaxing, when most of your professional appointments are in the evening, such an upside-down routine puts you in a different compartment.

There is a traditional antinomy in the work of the ministry. The *Decree on the Ministry and Life of Priests* says, 'They cannot be ministers of Christ unless they are witnesses and dispensers of a life other than this one' (art. 3). But it has *first* said, 'Presbyters are taken from among men and appointed for men in the things which pertain to God. . . Hence they deal with other men as brothers'. And immediately after the statement about 'dispensers of a life other than this', the Decree goes on, 'But they cannot be of service to men if they remain strangers to the life and condition of men'. The phrase 'a life other than this' I shall discuss later. For the moment let me say, what is very obvious, that the presbyter must not be so merged in the secular world that his religious role is wholly lost to view.

But there is the other principle that the presbyter is a 'brother' and 'no stranger'. For one and a half thousand years the stress has been on 'otherness'; a firm compensatory move in the other direction seems long overdue. I would like to make a few suggestions. The title 'Father' is often a sham. It implies that intimacy with people which Vatican II requires. But it seems nonsense to call a man 'Father' whose way of life is remote from your own, who dresses differently, perhaps has a different vocabulary, who may avoid appearing to have favourites in his congregation by being distant to all. In the mouths of some Catholics 'Father' rings very pleasantly. They make it a signal of warmth and trust. But most of the time it is a mask of differentiation and status. A lady was watching her priest brother-in-law cross the room with arms full of vestments. When he reached the door she sprang forward, 'Let me open the door, Pat', she said. The priest's sister looked up and felt obliged to repress this familiarity. 'Father Pat', she said incisively.

If 'Father' is mostly a mark of status, what are we to say about 'The Reverend' as a handle to a presbyter's name? Can you deal with men as a brother if you start off with the stipulation that they approach you with reverence! When young Joseph naively told his brothers that they were fated to reverence him, they were tempted to murder him. That reaction was extreme; but brothers are generally averse to showing much reverence.

Then we have clerical clothes. Can you deal with other

people as brothers if their first glimpse of you proclaims not your common humanity, but your difference of status and vocation? There is in this country a stereotype of the clergyman, 'the man of the cloth', 'the chap with the dog collar'. It does not start with an admission that we are fellow human beings. It is concerned with our oddity. And this stereotype is in varying degrees called into people's minds as soon as we appear.

On these grounds I decided to give up wearing clerical clothes. In practice, I wear them a good deal so as not to scandalise people to whom I have no opportunity of offering an explanation. The experience of not wearing clerical clothes is very interesting. I had no idea how rude so many people are to one another. Clerical dress had insulated me from this particular 'condition of man'. Of course, I am often told by people, some of them surprisingly young, that they 'like a priest to look like a priest'. The reason, though sometimes not admitted, is quite plain.

Most Catholics, if they have been talking to you for a while and then find out that you are a priest, are quite embarrassed, and often distinctly annoyed. One girl even thumped me, her irritation prevailing over her respect for the clergy. People are annoyed because they think they have been tricked into talking to you just as they would to anyone else. How on earth can I be said to be dealing with other men as brothers when I must wear some sort of signal to warn them to speak to me in a special way?

My researches have not yet established just how you should talk to a priest. Some people seem to think that we are sorely distressed at hearing a mild swear word. In a current ITV advert a young woman is aghast at having uttered a single expletive, albeit in a genteel and ladylike way, in front of the vicar. Then, I suppose, people are afraid that they will come out with worldly attitudes or unorthodox opinions which would distress the priest or lower his opinion of them. But what kind of brother am I, if people always have to be on their guard when talking to me? And am I not going to be a stranger to the life and condition of men if nobody ever speaks naturally to me?

The questions whether I should have the title 'Reverend', be called 'Father' and wear clerical clothes may seem practical details, not theological. But the Council's statement that we should deal with other men as 'brothers', that we should not be 'strangers to the life and condition of men' are part of a theological perspective. Conversely, the attitude that priests are different and that the difference should be marked by a title and distinctive dress, also implies a theological view, the one expressed, 'They cannot be ministers of Christ unless they are witnesses and dispensors of a life other than this'.

This whole matter might be seen as a practical question, the particular situation determining whether the principle of 'brotherhood' or the principle of 'difference' should prevail. Taking the issue in these terms I would urge that the principle of the 'difference' has had a very long innings and would do well to declare. But I think that a more radical solution is possible. I would presume to suggest that the phrase 'a life other than this earthly one' is a little clumsy. It is misleading to speak as though there were two lives, one 'earthly' and the other running concurrently and in parallel, which is supernatural and eternal. We have one life. At one level I am a vegetative process. At a deeper level I am capable of reflection and aesthetic appreciation, of moral choice. The Christian believes that the ultimate level, the final dimension of his life is his relationship with God. But the 'spiritual' life is not a separate entity. My body is from God. The Creed proclaims the resurrection of the body. Baptism and the receiving of the Eucharist are, in part, bodily events. So I would prefer to say that the presbyter is a witness not to 'another' life, but to the Christian vision of what this life is at its deepest level, its origin from God and its culmination with God. The presbyter then, must establish himself as a fellow human being if he is to carry conviction about the divine dimension of our lives. Christ plunged himself into the common life of men in order to bring his revelation. The presbyter should surely follow the same formula, and establish himself as a brother before he can become a witness to the divine dimension of human life. Once I spent a week in the hospital. When forms were being filled, I said that I was a teacher and an assistant chaplain. This was rendered 'R.C. Priest'. The sister, not a Catholic, came to me and said 'I know that you priests need privacy. I have no private ward. I could put you up a bed in the corner of the office.' Faithful to my theories, I politely declined. However, I don't think that I did very much to illuminate for my fellow patients the divine dimension of their lives. They were more impressed by the girl students who came to visit me.

One of the advantages of obligatory celibacy is that every Latin Catholic priest is born into a lay family and reared in a lay atmosphere. The process of clericalisation must be very intense to off-set our respectable lay origins! Clerical celibacy is now called in doubt. Vatican II affords no encouragement to those who want to change the discipline. The Council does state (*Decree on Priests*, 16) that celibacy is not demanded by the very nature of the priesthood. They could hardly say otherwise when the first generations of Christian ministers were married, as are the diocesan clergy of the Eastern rites today. Then the Council gives a number of reasons why celibacy is very fitting in a presbyter. I shall not rehearse their reasons, but they are eloquent enough almost to undermine the previous statement that celibacy is not demanded by the nature of the presbyterate. In fact, the Council seems to take the position that the presbyterate is quite compatible with matrimony, but celibacy is so desirable that it was, and is, quite right to make it compulsory for all presbyters of the Western Church. This is not wholly convincing. Are the circumstances of the Eastern and Latin churches so different that what is normal among the presbyters of one should be forbidden to the presbyterate of the other?

I would suggest that we have here a failure to recognise diversity of vocation, unless the different vocations are confined to different areas. The Church recognises a diversity of vocations in the Church as an axiom. But our practice often inclines to the monolithic. I was once very interested in a lay movement which undoubtedly inspired many Catholics to more purposeful Christian practice. But I had misgivings. The general formula of the movement was a diluted version of the spiritual practices of my own order, cut up small and easy for lay consumption, but nourishing all the same. In my unease, I went to a clever, shrewd, quite learned and highly practical diocesan priest. I asked if he could recommend a good book on lay spirituality. He promptly told me that such a book would be hard to find; there was not even a worth-while writing on the spirituality of the diocesan priest, because, he averred, the spiritual books were written by members of religious orders.

When one comes to think of it, the diocesan priest is a kind of half-monk, obliged to celibacy and the recitation of Office. The vigour of the monastic movement and the orders which developed from it may have distorted or impoverished the authentic vocations of diocesan clergy and laity. In the same simplifying, stereotyping way the Western tradition sees in practice only one form of presbyterate, the celibate.

A diversity of vocations can be hard to handle in practice. Even if the diocesan clergy are semi-monks, there are many problems about their relationship with the religious orders, whether it be the theoretical difficulty I indicated before about the bishop and the religious priest, or, at a more sordid level, jealousy and suspicion. It is always easier to standardise than to orchestrate differences. But if the latter is harder, it is far richer when successful.

Obligatory celibacy can be discussed at great length, and yet is often treated too cavalierly both by the conservatives who would see change as an ignominious surrender, and by radicals who often say that celibacy should be optional, and leave it at that. They overlook a whole tissue of practical considerations, the first of which, in my selection, would be that a married clergy would mean pastoral vocations coming in pairs. But this little work is concerned with principles, and I suggest that there are three; one: celibacy is not essential to the presbyterate; two: the charism of celibacy can be a great asset (cf. *The Decree on Priests*, 16); three: there are diversities of vocation within the Church and within the presbyterate

70

itself, differences as large as that between marriage and celibacy. To continue to confine the two vocations of married and celibate presbyter within different rites smacks more of standardisation than orchestration.

Chapter 9

CONCLUSION

Yesterday I was waiting outside a hospital ward when a kindly Free Church chaplain came up to me and introduced himself. Although I was not in clerical dress, he knew, he said, by my smile that I was some sort of minister. It is one of the most surprising things I have ever had said to me, and one of the most disconcerting. Do I, in spite of my melancholy disposition, have one of those ready, bland smiles, with an ambience of unfocussed benevolence? Perhaps the clerical smile would provide material for some interesting religio-sociological - physiognometrical research.

But we have a more serious, and I hope, more realistic project, which is to conclude our exploration of the nature of the priesthood. Conclusions are going to be rather elusive. For instance, I do not want to use the word 'priest', and that, in a work on the theology of the priesthood, is something of a snag. The word 'priest' is now encrusted with ceremonial associations so that the whole balance of the ministry is viewed distortedly. The word now serves to confuse the Christian minister with the Aaronic and gentile hierarchs, as though there were a basic similarity between the three categories. In origin 'presbyter' was a very unecclesiastical, non-cultic term. But its descendant, 'priest', seems irredeemably clericalised and over-sacerdotalised. I should like to speak of the 'minister'. But the bishop and the deacon, where he exists, are also ministers. So perhaps, like the early Christians, I shall make do with 'presbyter'.

A second reason why conclusions verge on the evanescent is that presbyters did not always fulfill exactly the same function. The presbyters of the New Testament worked with, under the direction of, the Apostles. Presumably the presbyters in Jerusalem working with James had one set of responsibilities, and the presbyters appointed by the migratory Paul, quite another. Some generations later when the bishops have emerged, the presbyters seem a sort of committee helping their president, the bishop, to manage the local church, and sometimes deputising for him liturgically. As the Church expanded the presbyters were given charge of outlying congregations. Finally when the bishop had to confine himself to general supervision, the day-to-day ministry of teaching, presiding at ceremonies and directing the laity became largely the routine charge of the presbyterate. Now these are all different, if related, situations. The Jacobite presbyter, the Pauline presbyter, the Ignatian committee man, the pastor in the suburbs a short walk from his bishop's 'cathedral', the fully fledged parish priest of later date. . . has this progression come to a permanent halt? Is the form of the presbyterate fixed for ever? Are no more mutations possible? Or is a certain plasticity part of the concept of the office? I suggest that it is, and that a rigid definition of the presbyterate would be a false one.

A third reason why conclusions may be evasive is that I intend to be honest. That sounds as though I were accusing my theological betters of dishonesty. What I would condemn in some of them is an inadequate sense of reality. A few months ago I read a very stimulating paper on the priesthood by an American priest. One of his phrases has remained very clearly in my mind. He described the priest as ordained among other purposes in order to 'coordinate the charisms of the community'. That is a good phrase for a valuable concept and is just the thing to arouse my suspicions. I enquired about the writer. He is a theological writer and lecturer, and of course he has no congregation. So the only charisms he has to coordinate are his own. Does it follow that he is not really a priest, or only partly functioning as one? Certainly not. He is quite rightly a presbyter in his own eyes and the eyes of others, even without a congregation of his own. But when you read his paper, you are led to envisage each presbyter as surrounded by his own little flock. This presumption is common. It suggests that a curate is not fully a presbyter, and that I, who have never had even a district in a parish wherein to coordinate charisms, have never really been a presbyter at all.

When one is trying to explain something, one has usually to leave out complications for the sake of clarity. In doing so, one can easily produce a neat, clear concept which is rather remote from the facts which it is supposed to be making intelligible. I cannot promise to bring all the complications of clerical life and work into my construction. I shall certainly try to avoid such near-fantasy as imagining every presbyter to be fitted out with his personal congregation from the day of his ordination.

There seems to me an obvious analogy between presbyteral ordination and the sacraments of baptism and confirmation. In varying ways all three sacraments commit someone to the Church; all three involve responsibilities to the Church, and acceptance by the Church of the baptizand, confirmand or ordinand into an enhanced relationship with herself. Each of the three sacraments marks the beginning of new ties between the recipient and the Church. But the beginning is not an absolute beginning. Baptism is not the beginning of a person's relationship to the Church. The adult (to keep it a little simpler — in spite of what I said in the last paragraph) baptizand already knows the Church and believes in the Church and wants the Church, or he would not normally present himself for baptism. The minister responsible for the baptism must satisfy himself conscientiously of the presence of these dispositions before he confers the sacrament.

What are the predispositions for presbyteral ordination? Do you remember my irrelevant-seeming Syrian village pastor? He was a man respected by the village as a good man; he was chosen by the village. He was a man already committed to Christian standards, and he was called to assume a new and more onerous responsibility for their maintenance. In the Pastoral Epistles Paul demands of Timothy and Titus that they find men of solid, tried Christian virtue and give them responsibility in their churches. Again we have the two elements, of commitment to Christianity and the call to an increased responsibility. In the revised Roman rite of ordination the Bishop asks, 'Do you know if they are worthy?' He is answered, 'Upon enquiry among the People of God and upon

75

recommendation of those responsible for their training, they have been found worthy.'

In the course of the Church's history many a man has been ordained with scandalously inadequate commitment to Christian standards. Arrogant, predatory, lecherous or slothful, or even all four together, the Church would uphold them as validly ordained, and recognised the validity of their later sacramental actions. But this recognition should not lead us to think of holiness in the presbyter as merely desirable and becoming. As a preacher and teacher of the word the vicious presbyter is not merely defective, he is a massive obstacle to belief; he is a source of darkness and confusion where he was meant to bring light. Also he is quite incapacitated to guide a Christian community. Too much has been made of the fact that a gravely sinful priest can say a valid Mass and pronounce a valid absolution. He was not ordained just to perform valid sacramental actions. That is to reduce him to the cultic ritualist. He is a minister of the gospel, called, as the ancient Gallican rite says, 'that he may show himself a presbyter by the dignity of his acts and the righteousness of his life.'

In the last sentence I have used the word 'called', and I have used it of the man already conspicuously committed to the Church and 'called' to further responsibilities on its behalf. In the Syrian village the community called their new pastor. In the Pastoral Epistles Timothy and Titus seem to be directed to do the calling. A summons of some sort seems to be a constituent element of the presbyterate. In the West, communities no longer choose their pastor. When I was a boy a 'vocation to the priesthood' was commonly spoken of as an inner prompting in the mind and heart of a young man. When I was studying theology the subjective element was very much played down, and 'vocation' explained legalistically, and, I thought, over-rationally in terms of fitness, 'right intention' and acceptance by ecclesiastical authority. But whether the 'call' comes from a community, from the episcopate or from an interior urging, it seems to me that the Spirit summons a man to become more deeply engaged in the work of the Church, to take a step which will not merely increase his commitment quantitatively, but transform it qualitatively.

Transform it into what? The mission of the Church is the responsibility of the whole Church. It is for all the Church to preserve Christ's teaching, and to bring to the human race generation by generation the effects of Christ's life among us. The mission is not simply to non-Christians, as though Christians were already perfect in their knowledge, understanding and following of Christ. There has to be an inner activity within the Church, by which Christians grow in their assimilation to Christ, correct their mistakes, repair their misdeeds and enrich their relationship with God and their fellow men. We are all responsible for our fellow Christians, and for the rest of the world. But this responsibility is not uniform and homogeneous. It never was. In the New Testament, if I may quote myself, we read of 'the twelve', of 'apostles', of the 'seven', of 'bishops', of 'elders', of deacons, of prophets, evangelists, pastors, teachers, miracle-workers, healers and helpers, of administrators and of speakers in tongues. And, as we have seen in Chapter Four, the rich variety of the apostolic age crystallised a few generations later into a simpler structure, with the offices of bishop, presbyter and deacon distinct from the general body of believers, and from each other.

One point must be made with emphasis. We shall not get very far if we think of 'the bishop' and 'the priest'. We must think in terms of the episcopate and the presbyterate. The bishop does not preside over his diocese in isolation. He is primarily a member of the 'episcopal college', as his consecration by several bishops symbolises. The work of one bishop in his diocese will look very much like that of another in his. Yet there are also coadjutors and auxiliaries, and bishops employed in the Vatican, and legates and delegates from the Vatican. All are undeniably bishops. They are not bishops because they have a titular see each, although the obstinate convention by which they are given one is quite interesting. Nor, at this stage, must we go back to saying they are bishops in that they confirm, ordain and consecrate, which a presbyter cannot do. They are all bishops because they have been consecrated members of the episcopate.

The activities of presbyters are more diverse than those of bishops. Besides the 'pastoral clergy' there are full-time workers in ecclesiastical administration, teachers of theology, directors of catechetical institutes, writers, editors, while at Castel Gandolfo six Jesuits observe the movements of the stars in their courses, feeding the results to their computer, discharging their often nocturnal task, I am told, in their stockinged feet, should His Holiness be in residence in the apartments below. What all these men have in common is not so much the practice of saying Mass or the power to hear confessions if called upon, but their membership in the presbyterate. This is the root whence spring their sacramental powers, whether they be used constantly or infrequently. I am not saying that once a man has been ordained into the presbyterate it does not matter how he spends his time. His membership commits him to direct his life by the purposes of the presbyterate. It is in direct pastoral work that that purpose is most obviously fulfilled, and I suspect that every presbyter worth his salt, or rather his dollop of anointing chrism, should he find himself called to ecclesiastical administration, teaching, or the care of the Pope's observatory, will always hanker in some degree after 'the care of souls' and feel a certain envy for his brethren 'in the parishes'. It is very necessary for our morale, for our spiritual health, that we see a clearly demonstrable connection between what we do and what we are, or, if you prefer polysyllables, between our occupations and the mission of the presbyterate.

On the subject of that mission, let us return to the *Decree on the Ministry and Life of Presbyters*. It says: 'Christ sent the Apostles just as He Himself had been sent by the Father. Through these same Apostles He made their successors, the bishops, sharers in His consecration and mission. Their ministerial role has been handed down to presbyters in a limited degree' (art.2). Two statements in that quotation must be taken in a highly qualified sense. The Apostles continued the work of Christ, but it would be blasphemous to say that their mission was absolutely identical with His. For instance, even if they were all martyred, they did not die for us in the same sense. Neither did the mission of the Twelve coincide in every detail with the responsibilities of Paul and James of Jerusalem. Nor must the phrase 'their successors', when used of the bishops, be taken to mean that a fully-fledged episcopacy was established before the deaths of the Apostles, waiting like the next member of a relay team, already in motion towards the goal, at the ready to receive the team baton. That 'their ministerial role has been handed down to the presbyters' is the least exceptionable, as it says nothing of the origin of the presbyterate, nor of the route by which their 'limited share' has come down to them.

I seem to be presenting a very inconclusive conclusion. One thing, however, seems to me to be incontrovertible: that responsibility in and for the Church is not uniform. One can raise questions about the term 'Twelve' and about the title 'Apostle'; but no-one can deny that the New Testament depicts the Twelve as having a special relationship to Christ, nor deny that the Apostles are represented as bearing a much heavier responsibility than that of the rank-and-file Christian. Their responsibility is to proclaim Christ, to gather together a community of those who accept that message and to guide that community. The administration of the sacraments, which has become for us the most conspicuous part of the ministry, is the least in evidence. At a later stage in history when the population was nominally Christian, the proclamation of the gospel receded in importance. So did the formation of the Christian community. It was already formed and required only maintenance work and the regular administration of the sacraments. The work of proclamation, of gathering Christians, became the specialised work of the missionary, while in Europe the clergy largely saw themselves, though in more impressive terms, as maintenance men. The result is horrifying.

Am I wrong in thinking that the bulk of the presbyterate, and equally of the episcopate, is now unable to speak to the non-Christian world in words that genuinely communicate? We seem to me to be unable to speak to the nominal, but non-practising, Christians, and even to quite a large section of the practising but doubting, in words that carry any conviction. I know that I myself was trained to minister to members of the Church, to give them the sacraments, to expound to them the faith they already had, to guide to a more exemplary Christian practice those who were already reasonably proficient. Although a little hazy about recent changes in the ceremonies, I can administer the sacraments both validly and decently. I can preach competently to a congregation of 'good Catholics' and I have sometimes given effective retreats to religious and devout lay people. And in the open unbelieving world I might as well be a mentally handicapped child, for all I have to say to it. I know that I can generalise from my own condition to that of the clergy in general, thanks to the standardisation of seminary studies. A dozen years ago a number of pregnant women took the drug thalidomide, and we now have a group of eleven-year-old children with malformed limbs. For generations we thought of the priest primarily as a Mass-sayer and a pastor of thoroughly domesticated sheep. Because we have absorbed that quite erroneous concept into our system, we have now bred a defective and malformed presbyterate, incompetent as regards the primary responsibility of the Church, and the first charge upon her ministry, the proclamation of the gospel.

The theologian to whom I was a little unkind on the subject of coordinating charisms sees the responsibility of the ministry to possess four facets: the proclamation of the gospel (*kerygma*); the formation and development of the community (*koinonia*); the service of the world (*diakonia*); and worship (*eucharistia*). About the first, second and fourth of these facets there can be no argument, and I certainly would not want to argue against the third, but I doubt whether I could establish it. The principal service which we have to offer the world is the preaching of the gospel, and that comes under the first heading of kerygma. The first Christians showed great concern for the poor, but they would seem to be the poor of their own community, who probably absorbed all their resources. Certainly the *Constitution On The Church* says, 'she recognises in the poor and the suffering the likeness of her poor and suffering Founder' (art.8). But does this implementation of the gospel message constitute a distinct facet of the Church's mission?

Perhaps that discussion is purely academic. Find in it three aspects or four, the responsibility imparted to the Apostles was clearly on a different plane from that of the mass of Christians. What was transmissible of that responsibility, and not everything was, became the responsibility of the episcopate. To speak of the episcopate 'handing down' a limited share of this ministerial role makes them sound like elder brothers dealing with their old clothes. The Apostles were assisted by 'elders', by 'overseers', a seemingly amorphous class whose functions probably varied according to place and circumstance. From this class arose the bishops, rising, as it were, to the occasion of the demise of the Apostles, while the mass of elders, or rather their successors, continued to give the bishops more or less the help they had given the Apostles. The presbyters play a supporting role. Their responsibility for proclamation, community, service and worship is a subordinate responsibility. This does not mean that they are mere amplifiers or rediffusion agencies of the local bishop enabling his activities to reach into areas where the restrictions of time and place prevent his personal presence. Normally the presbyter requires a mission from the local bishop to preach, to help a local community, to administer the sacraments. But the presbyter's mission is fundamentally from the Church as a whole and for the ends of the Church. If a bishop were to teach manifest heresy in his pastorals, the presbyters would be obliged to refuse to promulgate them. If a bishop were to take a flagrantly unchristian line in political or social issues, the presbyterate would not only be entitled to withhold their cooperation, they would be obliged to protest. This is not to say that the presbyterate are the appointed censors of their diocesan, but that as 'prudent' cooperators they have to use their own discernment, as 'counsellors' they must develop their own powers of judgement. Their *raison d'etre* is not merely the service of the local bishop, but the service of the Church. Their mission is the Church's mission, which they normally implement by working with and for the local bishop, but which they may have to fulfil in spite of him, should he prove unfaithful to that mission.

Because the presbyter is not merely an assistant of the local diocesan, some presbyters may be working at a national or international project. The occupations of the presbyterate are, and ought to be, very diverse. The mission of the Church calls for the use of every means in our power; it involves a variety of approaches and tactics. It is to the obvious advantage of the presbyterate that its ranks should include a rich variety of experience, provided that experience is properly pooled. All presbyteral activity should be directed to the four-(three-?)fold mission of the Church, of proclamation, of building and fostering the Christian community, of serving the world, of worship. And as the responsibility of the presbyterate for this mission is a subordinate one, the activities of the presbyterate should be pursued in harmony with, and under the direction of, the episcopate, with the Bishop of Rome at its head.

I spoke of the responsibility of the Apostles as being on a different plane from that of the other Christians. It would be convenient to speak of the responsibility of the episcopacy being on one plane, that of the presbyterate on another, and, dodging the issue of the diaconate, the responsibility of the laity on a third. But planes are normally imagined as higher and lower with overtones of status and rank, which this age finds uncongenial. The mission of the Church bears upon every member of the Church. The layman is charged with the proclamation of the gospel, even if it be by the wholly silent eloquence of a Christian life. He must be a source of strength to the Christian community, of assistance to the world, and play his part in the Church's worship. These are all positive activities, not passive roles. Yet the quality, the intensity, of the bishop's responsibility for the people of his diocese is undoubtedly of a different order from the responsibility of the layman for his neighbour's 'soul'. So, too, the responsibility of the presbyter for the instruction, the pastoral guidance and sacramental life of the community is of another degree from that of the lay member.

The matter is complex. My own religious instruction owes more to the mistresses of my primary school than to the parish clergy, which is not to say that the clergy should have been giving the religious instruction classes. A devoted, veteran layman may impart more momentum to the community life of the parish than the inexperienced curate. It is on liturgical occasions that the distinction between presbyter and layman is clearest, which is one reason why the presbyter has so often been defined in terms of his liturgical role, a mistake we must not perpetuate. Yet the liturgical role of the presbyter does recapitulate his general role. Liturgically he leads; in the homily he should lead the congregation to a deeper knowledge and practice of the gospel; he leads in the action which they are performing as a community; he leads them in the act of worship. His responsibility is plainly different from that of the congregation. The burden of initiative lies with him; it is for him to reach out to all, to carry them forward in understanding of the gospel, in growing together, in readiness to serve the world, in worship. I know that I myself find an active and alert congregation more tiring than the passive observers. When the congregation has taken part in the homily, when they have composed bidding prayers, when they have sung with a will, when they have been attentive and responsive throughout, they may well emerge bubbling, while I am quite flat. It goes without saying that the part of a congregation is by no means passive. You can explain only to actively receptive minds; you can bring together effectively only those who are willing to be together, ready to grow together; you can lead in worship only those who keep their hearts and minds raised to God. The members of the congregation have a responsibility not only for themselves, but to each other. They must help one another by putting themselves into the celebration and doing so in a way that will assist and not deter. Once again, there is a manifest difference between the responsibility of the minister for the congregation and the responsibility of the members to one another.

On liturgical occasions the minister wears vestments. It would be utterly pagan to think that certain apparel gives a man power, or that garments of a certain texture, quality or shape are intrinsically more apt for divine worship than others. At the early Christian gatherings there would have been no hieratic vestments. With an intelligent, well informed congregation it is possible without real loss, if not without rubrical offence, to dispense with them. They do have their uses. They mark the solemnity of the occasion; they indicate the distinctive responsibility of the minister; they associate the event visibly with the many liturgical occasions elsewhere in the present, and at other times in the past when such vestments have been worn. In so doing they bring out another aspect of the ministry. As a formally accredited representative of the Church the presbyter forms a bond between the particular liturgical assembly and the whole diocese, because of his relationship to the bishop. He is a bond between the particular assembly and the whole Church, because he is a member of the presbyterate which is linked with the whole episcopate. He links the particular congregation with the Church of the past, present and the future, because he has been ordained into the Church's enduring ministry.

'Thou art a priest for ever according to the order of Melchizedek', Cardinal Manning used to intone at his clergy by way of impressing on them their status and obligations. The reference to Melchizedek I find sonorous rather than illuminating, but I think that he did well to suggest the enduring nature of the presbyterate, the permanence of the membership and the time-transcending quality of their office. When I use the word 'enduring' I do not mean to imply rigidity. Rather the contrary, because the rigid is less fitted to endure than the flexible. I have already said that some degree of plasticity seems to be an essential of the presbyterate, and there is no reason at all to think that it has now reached its final and unchangeable form. It is much more reasonable to expect in a rapidly changing world the emergence of new forms, and we should be alert to their beginnings and foster their development.

Is one of these forms to be the woman-presbyter? This question could have come in the last chapter as one of the unsolved problems. Not everyone finds it unsolved. For the intransigently conservative it does not arise. For many 'progressives' it has already been solved, and the affirmative solution taken its place in the progressive credo. I suggest that we should approach the question in the following way: In the eucharistic liturgy the Church has always used bread and wine. She believes that in the course of the Mass the bread and wine undergoes that change which for centuries has been labelled 'transubstantiation'. What if tomorrow I were to use potatoes and milk? Would the same change take place? It is undoubtedly within God's power to effect it. Yet have we any guarantee that he would do so? Fortunately there is no reason to employ potatoes and milk, and I shall confidently use the customary hosts — not that they look much like bread — and wine. But what of those areas where wheaten bread is never eaten, where the vine does not grow and wine is never drunk? Are not bread and wine there quite unsuitable material for the eucharist? Have they not lost their character as staple food and drink? Would the substitution of say, rice and some local distillation, not be entirely valid? Could we not in such circumstances proceed with the local equivalents of bread and wine, confident that we are offering a valid mass? Has the Church the right to make such changes? Is it perhaps her duty to do so? Would it perhaps be less of a change to use ordinary local foodstuffs than the exotic materials which, in such changed circumstances, bread and wine have become?

So far the material of the Eucharist has been restricted to bread and wine and the material of the ordained ministry confined to male mankind. Is either restriction absolute? In some climates bread and wine are meaningless. Changes in the social climate are making it perfectly normal for women to exercise public responsibility equally with men. Should we not in certain geographical climates drop one restriction, and in a changed social climate, the other? I must admit that whereas the variation in eating habits is quite evident, the change in the social climate is, as yet, very partial. Everywhere public responsibility is predominantly in male hands. Three women prime ministers might seem to indicate otherwise, but of these one is a prime minister's widow, and another a male prime minister's daughter. In one respect my parallel is faulty. Dietary habits, cannibalism apart, are morally neutral. The social climate is not. Changes in the latter are not something which the Church should passively await; she should try to influence them in the right direction. The relevant questions then are: Has it been necessary symbolically and sacramentally to restrict the presbyterate to the male sex because among the Jews, and predominantly in most societies, public responsibility was a male preserve? If so, should not a change in society in this respect affect the conditions of the sacrament of Order? Should the Church precede rather than follow society in the matter? There is also the more fundamental question, whether the Church considers that she has the power to make such changes.

Perhaps I should have been less lightly dismissive about Melchizedek three paragraphs back. The Letter to the Hebrews mentions him with awe half a dozen times, and it is the Letter to the Hebrews which deals eloquently with the priesthood of Christ. Here I am using the word 'priest' in its traditional sense with all its associations of sanctuary and sacrifice. This concept of priesthood has so often distorted our understanding of the Christian ministry that I have preferred to keep it apart from the mainstream of my exposition. It is certainly outside the mainstream of New Testament thought. We have seen that the term used of Jewish and Gentile 'priests' was never applied in the New Testament to any office in the Christian community. Neither is Jesus ever described by the gospels as claiming to be a priest in the contemporary, cultic, sacrificial sense, although there may be sacerdotal overtones in some of his messianic statements. Nor do the other New Testament writings apply the term 'priest' in the Jewish sense to Christ, the Letter To The Hebrews being the great exception, because it does so repeatedly and resonantly. The great impediment here is that Jesus was not of Levitical descent. The writer trumps this difficulty by playing Melchizedek, applying Ps 110.4 to Jesus. Melchizedek to whom Abraham paid tithes and from whom he received a blessing was greater than Abraham and therefore than Levi and his race (7.4ff). Jesus represents mankind because he is a man: 'we have not a high priest who is unable to sympathise with our weakness, but one who in every respect has been tempted as we are' (4.14). He is appointed by God (5.5) and 'designated by God a high priest' (5.10). He offered 'prayers and supplications' (5.7); 'he entered once for all into the Holy Place, taking not the blood of goats and calves, but his own blood, thus securing an eternal redemption' (9.12); 'he holds his priesthood permanently, because he continues for ever' (7.23). His sacrifice is also permanent: 'by a single offering he has perfected for all time those who are sanctified' (10.14). It is beyond doubt that the writer is not speaking metaphorically when he describes Jesus as a high priest. He is at too great pains to establish Jesus' priesthood and to prove that priesthood superior to its Levitical predecessor. 'Christ has obtained a ministry which is as much more excellent than the old as the covenant he mediates is better' (8.6).

St Paul used hieratic language of himself and his work in the Letter to the Romans '. . . the grace given me by God to be a minister of Christ Jesus to the Gentiles in the priestly service of the gospel of God, so that the offering of the Gentiles may be acceptable' (15.15). The words strike one as being an eloquent metaphor rather than a formal claim to sacerdotal status. An interesting application of sacerdotal concepts from the Old Testament is the use made both in Peter's First Epistle (2.9), and in Revelation more than once (1.6 and 5.10 and perhaps 20.6) of the phrase a 'kingdom of priests', which figures originally in the promise made in Exodus (19.6): '. . . you shall be to me a kingdom of priests and a holy nation'. The phrase used of Israel in Exodus is applied to the new Christian community in both documents. Eventually, as we have already seen, in the post-Apostolic period sacrificial and sacerdotal phraseology occurs. Eventually it became the normal vocabulary in the description of the Church's most venerated action, the Eucharist, and the ministers who presided thereat.

If because of its antiquity and the solidly traditional use made of it in the Church, we wish to apply the Old Testament category of priesthood, there are solid justifications for doing so. The Aaronic priest was a man specially set aside and consecrated for his work, the principal part of which was ritual performance of the sacrifices, together with other ceremonies. The Letter to the Hebrews urges that the Jewish notion of priesthood is verified and surpassed in Jesus, and Israel's cultic ritual utterly transcended by his life, death and ascension. The Church is a human society; it is a special society distinct from the rest of the world; it has been anointed for its mission by the descent of the Spirit; it is the instrument by which the highpriestly work of Christ reaches successive generations of mankind. This 'priesthood of the Church' is essentially something dependent and partial. It is a derived and limited participation in the priesthood of Christ, which is unique, eternal and all-sufficient. As the mission of the Church is the mission of the whole Church, so the priesthood of the Church belongs to the whole Church. As the responsibility for the mission of the Church is variously distributed, so the priesthood of the Church is diversely exercised. The highest degree of responsibility for the discharge of the Church's mission lies with the episcopate; theirs too, is the highest order of the priesthood. The presbyterate, charged with its own role in the Church's mission, has its own appropriate participation in the priesthood of the Church. This priesthood of the presbyterate is most profoundly exercised on that occasion when the gospel is most solemnly proclaimed, when the community is most formally assembled, i.e. at the liturgical representation of the sacrifice of the Eternal High Priest.

This style of language has its pitfall. Because the Old Testament comes first in time, we are tempted to take its categories as the norm with which the New Testament categories are to be compared. But it is the New Testament, even though it is later in time, which is fundamental, which is the exemplar, which is normative. We should not ask whether an institution in the Church fulfils the nature of the Old Testament institution. We should start with the New

Testament person, institution or concept, and ask to what extent it is prefigured in the Old Testament. To see the Christian presbyter as the Aaronic priest in a later context is to get him badly out of focus.

One last point. Responsibility in the Church is solemnly conferred. We become members of the Church at baptism and fully constituted members at confirmation. Man and wife become so in the ceremony of marriage. The presbyter is ritually ordained. Yet alongside the need for the external, ceremonial, symbolic conferment of the sacrament we recognise the validity of 'baptism of desire' for those who are prevented from undergoing the ritual. Can one doubt that a baptized Christian, inculpably unconfirmed, if consistently required by circumstances to show the dedication of a mature Christian, would both be obliged to rise to the challenge, and strengthened or 'confirmed' to meet it? Suppose a remote Christian community, through no fault of its own both deprived of priests and cut off from the rest of the Church. Should those people not appoint a man, or men, to give the community leadership and direction, and to take the initiative in preserving, and perhaps deepening, their Christianity? Would not such a community, once it became clear that they would continue in this isolation for a very long time, be entitled to celebrate the Eucharist, with those appointed to lead the community presiding thereat?

Yet it seems to me that such men would not be fully presbyters. They would have the care of the community (coordinating its charism?), they would be responsible for the preservation and transmission of the gospel, and perhaps these tasks would carry with them the prerogative of full eucharistic presidency. Still lacking, I suggest, would be the status of formally accredited representatives of the Church. Ordination constitutes a man solemnly and explicitly a member of the Church's ministry in the rank of presbyter. The episcopal mission which supervenes on ordination, i.e. the appointment of a presbyter by a bishop to some work, reinforces the presbyter's representative quality. This, I think quite important dimension of the presbyteral office, would be lack-

89

ing in the hypothetical leaders of my imagined community. They would represent their own community; they would in a sense represent the universal Church to that community, but they would have to do both without formal appointment by, without explicit accreditation from, the Church *via* the episcopate.

My isolated, priestless community may seem rather unreal. It is a hypothetical case. Yet it serves, I think, to bring out the nature of the presbyterate, to do which has been all my endeavour.

BIBLIOGRAPHICAL NOTE

In this dissertation I have borrowed a good deal from David N. Power, *Ministers Of Christ And His Church* (Chapman, 1969), from J. A. Möhler, *The Origin And Evolution Of The Priesthood* (Alba House, 1970) and from four articles by Seamus Ryan in the *Irish Theological Quarterly* for 1965 and 1966. I found *'Qu'est-ce qu'un prêtre'* by R. Salaun and Marcus (Editions du Seuil, 1965) quite stimulating. On the New Testament evidence Raymond Brown, *Priest And Bishop* (Paulist Press, 1970) was very helpful, as was also *Concilium*, Vol. 4, No. 8, on *Ecumenism*.

The Ninth Downside Symposium on *The Christian Priesthood* (D. L. & T., 1971) contains much scholarship, valuable insights and information and, for my money, some eccentric comment. The pamphlet, *What Priesthood Has The Ministry?* by Jean Tillard (Grove Books, 1973) should not be missed. I was helped by Piet Fransen in *Intelligent Theology, Vol. 2* (D. L. & T., 1968), and by 'Priest Or Presbyter' in *Authority in a Changing Church* (Sheed and Ward, 1968) by Nicholas Lash.

INDEX